S0-ARK-267

Deacons As Leaders

Robert Sheffield,
Compiler and Contributer

© Copyright 1991
Reprinted 1996, 1998, 2001

Convention Press

All rights reserved.

ISBN 0-7673-1956-7

This book is a text for course number LS-0100
for the Advanced Deacon Ministry Diploma
of the Christian Growth Study Plan.

Dewey Decimal Number 262.1
Subject Area: DEACONS

Printed in the United States of America.

LifeWay Church Resources
a division of LifeWay Christian Resources
of the Southern Baptist Convention
127 Ninth Avenue North
Nashville, Tennessee 37234

Contents

4 | Preface

5 | Chapter 1
Deacons Modeling Biblical Leadership
Charles W. Deweese

20 | Chapter 2
Deacons Leading in Church Ministry
Charles Warnock III

34 | Chapter 3
Deacons Leading in Community Ministry
Gary Hardin

48 | Chapter 4
Deacons Leading as Change Agents
Robert Sheffield

65 | Chapter 5
Deacons Leading in Times of Transition
Charles Belt

81 | Chapter 6
Deacons Leading with Pastor and Staff
Jerry Songer

Preface

Robert Sheffield

Deacons serve in vital leadership positions in the church. This is true from a biblical as well as practical standpoint. Unfortunately, deacons, pastors, and church members have not always understood or appreciated the role of deacon leadership. The nature of deacon leadership and the scope of deacon ministry have often been misunderstood in the life of the church.

Deacons As Leaders seeks to clarify the nature of deacon leadership. Space does not permit us to cover every area where deacons express leadership. The subjects covered represent critical areas of concern for you, your fellow deacons, and your entire church.

The writers of *Deacons As Leaders* bring knowledge, experience, and insight into their chapters. Their comments will broaden your understanding concerning deacon leadership.

To gain full benefit from this book, consider the following study process. First, read the book through carefully and prayerfully. Underline significant sentences and words. Then read it a second time. Carefully reflect upon the underlined points. Let them impact your mind and heart. Finally, discuss the book with other deacons.

Deacons As Leaders was written for you. It is my prayer that this book will enable you to become a more effective deacon for the glory of our Lord and the growth of His church.

1
Deacons Modeling Biblical Leadership

Charles W. Deweese

Charles W. Deweese is executive director-treasurer, Southern Baptist Historical Society, Brentwood, Tennessee, and currently serves as deacon chairman, First Baptist Church, Nashville, Tennessee.

Not every lemon is sour. Joel B. Lemon, Baptist deacon, proved that through his effective leadership.[1] For 33 years (1861-94), he served as deacon in the Mill Creek Baptist Church in Botetourt County, Virginia. Spanning the Civil War and Reconstruction, his life as deacon reflected important leadership traits and achievements.

As an active participant in Mill Creek's Sunday School, Lemon studied the Bible faithfully, learning principles of biblical leadership along the way. He then modeled what he learned by serving from time to time as church treasurer, moderator, trustee, pulpit committee member, discipline committee member, and messenger to the Valley Baptist Association. He also arranged hospitality for church guests, visited absent members, urged members to contribute toward the church's financial needs, supported mission causes outside the church, and served on a committee charged to send food and other provisions to Richmond College.

Lemon was also a loving husband, a caring father, and a community-minded citizen. He and his wife reared a large family of sons and daughters, of whom all received a basic education and several graduated from college. Two sons became Baptist ministers, and one became a physician. In 1870 Lemon helped form one of the first public schools in Virginia. He strongly supported the building and maintaining of roads in Botetourt County.

Times have changed. Deacons today do not tend to serve lengthy terms; instead, they usually serve short terms on a rotating basis. And deacons today do not necessarily serve as church treasurers, moderators, or trustees, or in other aspects of church administration; instead, they function more fully as servants in the pastoral ministries of the church. However, at least one key Baptist conviction links Joel Lemon and deacons today: leadership in personal, family, church, work, and community life is vital to deacon effectiveness. And such leadership must evolve from and relate to biblical models and principles of leadership.

Deacon Leadership is Essential

In ordination a church recognizes the leadership a deacon has already expressed as a Christian disciple, affirms its confidence in the deacon's potential for increased leadership, and states its expectation that the deacon will accept and mirror biblical patterns of leadership. Therefore, ordination implies that a deacon can serve Christ and the church best as a leader.

Effective deacon leadership is essential to creative patterns of lay ministry, to the quality of a church's worship, to covenantal relationships that tie a church together, to the moral and spiritual tone that a church sets, and to the successful completion of a church's overall tasks.

The Baptist stress on the priesthood of all believers affirms that ministry belongs to the whole church. Baptists elect deacons hoping that they will minister by leading all church members to engage in practical discipleship.

Baptists continue to assign specific leadership roles to their deacons as they have done for centuries. Why? One important reason is the biblical mandate that "everything should be done in a fitting and orderly way" (1 Cor. 14:40, NIV)[2]. Second, the congregational form of church government requires strong leadership.

Third, a church's need to carry out its calling and mission compels it to place deacons in the forefront of service-oriented leadership.

In 1987-88, I served as chairman of deacons at Judson Baptist Church in Nashville, Tennessee. That experience convinced me that the Lord, the Bible, and the church have a right to expect that deacons lead by expressing vision, taking courageous ethical stands, seeking to meet the spiritual standards of the Bible, preserving vital Christian traditions, making creative and flexible adjustments to change, using crisis as a time for learning, and cultivating the varying gifts of church members.

That experience also taught me that every person who agrees to be ordained as a deacon should be prepared to be viewed as a leader. Church members automatically assume that their deacons will be good leaders, even if the deacons do not absorb leadership into their self-identity. The potential danger of confused identity is that deacons may lose the respect of the church. The advantage of a healthy self-understanding regarding leadership is that deacons can help guide the church into meaningful patterns of ministry.

Deacon Leadership is Biblical

Three ideals—freedom, cooperation, and accountability—best describe the biblical style of leadership for deacons. The Bible invites deacons to maximize their individual gifts of leadership, urges them to cooperate in achieving the mission of the church, and stresses their accountability to God and the congregation.

Strong deacon leadership grows out of biblical requirements. Robert Sheffield's book *The Ministry of Baptist Deacons* contains a valuable chapter on "Deacons Ministering as Christian Leaders." This chapter highlights character qualities which the Bible expects of anyone desiring to lead. These qualities include servanthood, commitment, faith, vision, perseverance, and enthusiasm.[3]

Why is it so important that deacons turn to the Bible as the main source for their leadership style? Quite simply, Baptists view the Bible as the sole written authority for their faith and practices. First Timothy 3 presents excellent qualifications for deacon leaders. But we can search the entire Bible for valid principles and models of leadership for deacons. Eight such principles follow.

1. *Effective deacons lead by living daily under the lordship of Christ.*—Peter stated in his sermon on the Day of Pentecost: "Therefore let all Israel be assured of this: God has made this Jesus, whom you crucified, both Lord and Christ" (Acts 2:36, NIV). Philippians 2:11, part of an early Christian hymn, urges that "every tongue confess that Jesus Christ is Lord, to the glory of God the Father" (NIV). The confession that "Jesus is Lord" quickly became one of the favorite claims of early Christians.

The lordship of Christ means that all people owe Christ absolute obedience. The integrity of deacon leadership rises to or falls on the basis of its commitment to Christ as Lord. Deacons devoted to the lordship of Christ possess changed priorities, values, and dreams. Put simply, they behave and believe differently than before. They read the Sermon on the Mount with new understanding. They imitate the life of Christ with increased intensity. They accept their ministry roles as Christian servants with fresh zeal. They worship with higher motivation.

A deacon who leads under the lordship of Christ gains a clearer perspective of the importance of the things of this world. This kind of deacon has been "born again" by the Holy Spirit (John 3:3,7, NIV), has received "baptism into death" (Rom. 6:4, NIV), has become "a new creation" (2 Cor. 5:17, NIV), and "overcomes the world" (1 John 5:4, NIV). Equipped with these New Testament credentials, any deacon magnifies the possibility of making a major impact as a church and community leader.

Devotion to the lordship of Christ guarantees freedom. Acceptance of the obligation to subject oneself to Christ in all things frees a deacon to abandon self-reliance, to lead with imagination, to point the church toward its high calling from God, and to serve with joy. Paul's warning and encouragement to the Galatians goes to the heart of deacon leadership: "You, my brothers, were called to be free. But do not use your freedom to indulge the sinful nature; rather, serve one another in love" (5:13, NIV).

Hymns of our faith express the lordship of Christ in powerful ways. Such hymns include "All Hail the Power," "Come, Thou Almighty King," "Crown Him with Many Crowns," "Fairest Lord Jesus," "Have Thine Own Way, Lord," and "Jesus Is Lord of All." Through singing these hymns, deacons affirm their dependency upon Christ, worship with the people whom they are called to lead, and then lead with the awareness that service, not control, is the central motif of their ministry.

2. *Effective deacons lead by committing themselves to the historic purposes of the church.*—Acts 6:5 identifies seven men chosen by the early church to assist in the daily distribution of food to Grecian widows. Although Acts does not designate these men as deacons, their assignment "to wait on tables" (6:2, NIV) comes from the same root as the Greek word *diakonos* which can be translated into English as deacon or servant. Philip was one of the seven.

When persecution broke out against the church in Jerusalem, Philip "went down to a city in Samaria and proclaimed the Christ there" (8:5, NIV). Adversity seemed to deepen his dedication to the church. Acts 8 depicts Philip in the multiple roles of preacher, healer, evangelist, and teacher. Because of his preaching, "spirits came out of many, and many paralytics and cripples were healed" (8:7, NIV). With excitement, when many "believed Philip as he preached the good news of the kingdom of God and the name of Jesus Christ, they were baptized, both men and women" (8:12, NIV). Later, on a desert road to Gaza, Philip assumed the roles of evangelist and teacher in relating to an Ethiopian eunuch, resulting in the eunuch's conversion and baptism (8:26-38).

The model set by Philip in Acts 6 and 8 urges today's deacons to accept appropriate responsibility for leading the church to stay close to the purposes for which Christ created it. Since the church exists to share the good news of Christ, deacons need to bear a meaningful verbal and life-style witness and to undergird mission work. Since the church exists to glorify God and enjoy fellowship with Him, deacons need to worship weekly with fellow Christians. Since the church exists to teach the content and disciplines of the faith, deacons need to participate faithfully in Sunday School, Discipleship Training, and other educational opportunities of church life. Since the church exists to meet human need, deacons need to invest themselves in family ministry programs and other pastoral ministries of the church.

Helping the church understand and attain its New Testament calling penetrates the heart of deacon leadership. Respected by a congregation, deacons occupy a unique position of service from which to lead church members to upgrade and protect the regenerate nature of church life. They can do this by leading them to meet biblical requirements for doctrinal soundness, moral purity, spiritual growth, covenant relationship, and active ministry.

3. *Effective deacons lead by engaging daily in personal devotions and family worship.*—Personal Bible study and prayer provide a strong foundation for deacon leadership. Viewing the Bible as the primary source of Christian faith and practice and of spiritual inspiration, deacons who read the Bible daily can eventually say with the psalmist both that "I have hidden your word in my heart that I might not sin against you" (119:11, NIV), and that "Your word is a lamp to my feet and a light for my path" (119:105, NIV). Thus prepared, deacons can lead with confidence, courage, and humility.

Bold praying also characterizes the private lives of deacons who lead out of a sense of biblical calling. Daniel 6 presents a remarkable example of personal prayers in a difficult time. King Darius approved a law to throw into a den of lions anyone who prayed within 30 days to any god or man, except to Darius himself. Knowing that he might wind up in a den of lions, Daniel refused to let a government ruler dictate the nature of his prayer life. Following the routine pattern of his life, he responded courageously: "Now when Daniel learned that the decree had been published, he went home to his upstairs room where the windows opened toward Jerusalem. Three times a day he got down on his knees and prayed, giving thanks to his God, just as he had done before" (v. 10, NIV). Regular prayer enables deacons to commune with God, worship God, and commit themselves to God. These actions and attitudes add depth, maturity, and substance to deacon leadership.

Deacons who model biblical leadership also engage in daily family worship. The 1837 Circular Letter of the Old Colony Baptist Association in Massachusetts focused on the importance of family worship. Citing biblical support for the practice, the letter viewed family worship as important because it strengthened parental influence over children, offered a valuable setting for Christian instruction, and prepared family members for Christian service.[4] Deacons who lead by ministering to other people's families need first to be ministers to their own. Baptists have long recognized that biblical ideal. They have rightly stressed that "a deacon must be the husband of but one wife and must manage his children and his household well" (1 Tim. 3:12, NIV).

4. *Effective deacons lead by responding enthusiastically to God's will for their lives.*—John the Baptist typified this principle in a wonderful way. When "the word of God came to John son of Zechariah in the desert," immediately "he went into all the country around the Jordan, preaching a baptism of repentance for the forgiveness of sins" (Luke 3:2-3, NIV). Isaiah 40:3-5 had anticipated that John would respond excitedly to his call from God, and the angel Gabriel had expressed this anticipation to Zechariah (Luke 1:11-17).

Jesus expects all His disciples to follow Him. Simon and Andrew, the first two disciples whom He called, modeled the proper Christian response to their invitation to leadership roles: "At once they left their nets and followed Him" (Mark 1:18, NIV). Captivated by their new relationship with Christ and the possibilities of ministry tied to it, they set the pace for all future Christian leaders, including deacons, by quickly accepting Christ's calling. And they responded this way without knowing either the full demands of Christ for their lives or what the future would hold.

Baptist deacons occupy pivotal leadership roles in church life. Zeal, fervor, and optimism about their calling need to complement their ordination. Positive attitudes about leadership opportunities affect church members' perceptions of deacons. When the congregation senses that deacons have accepted their leadership enthusiastically and are using it responsibly, the members then view deacons as dynamic contributors to the church. Respect and support for deacon leadership soon follow.

William Carey, father of the modern mission movement, launched his career in the early 1790s as English Baptists' first foreign missionary after inviting those Baptists to "expect great things from God; attempt great things for God." That spirit of anticipation saturated Carey's leadership style throughout his magnificent missionary work in India. In reacting to God's call, he listened attentively, prayed expectantly, and responded committedly. Carey's vibrant devotion to God's will provides a major message for today's deacons.

5. *Effective deacons lead by encouraging, motivating, equipping, and serving others.*—These patterns of service and leadership permeated Jesus' self-understanding. Soon after overcoming three temptations presented to Him by the devil, Jesus set the stage for and established the meaning of His ministry by entering the synagogue in Nazareth and reading from a scroll of the prophet Isaiah: " 'The Spirit of the Lord is on me, because he has anointed me to preach good news to the poor. He has sent me to proclaim freedom for the prisoners and recovery of sight for the blind, to release the oppressed, to proclaim the year of the Lord's favor' " (Luke 4:18-19, NIV).

Jesus' encounter with Zacchaeus (Luke 19:1-10) vividly illustrates how He changed a life through a ministry of support. He encouraged Zacchaeus by inviting him to come down from a sycamore-fig tree so that He could go to his house and spend some time with him. He motivated Zacchaeus by leading him to evaluate the moral and spiritual aspects of his life. He equipped him with a new sense of purpose by leading him to accept the salvation which only He could offer. He served this wealthy tax collector by guiding him to confess that he would give half of his possessions to the poor and that he would repay four times any amount that he had cheated from anyone.

Jesus is the ultimate model for deacons. His first-century commitment to meeting the needs of others speaks volumes to the responsibilities of deacons today. He calls deacons to imitate Him. He pleads for deacons to care for people where they hurt. He urges deacons to view love for neighbor as an essential quality of leadership in church and community life. Jesus' call for each of His disciples to "take up his cross and follow me" (Matt. 16:24, NIV) includes deacons. And that call requires a self-denying approach to Christian service.

Deacon leadership implies a willingness to invest oneself in the needs of others. To illustrate, during a recession in the mid-1970s, many residents of Candler, North Carolina, experienced industrial work layoffs or had their hours cut back. Deacons in the Hominy Baptist Church in Candler responded by forming a Deacon Economic Assistance Committee (DEAC) to assist church members facing severe economic problems.[5] Deacons who serve in that kind of way discover the true meaning of Christian leadership.

6. *Effective deacons lead by assessing ministries needing to be done, setting goals for achieving them, developing strategies, mobilizing resources, working cooperatively, and expressing thanksgiving to God for positive results.*—Nehemiah demonstrated mastery of all these leadership skills and attitudes as he coordinated the rebuilding of the walls around Jerusalem in the fifth century B.C.

After obtaining permission from King Artaxerxes to travel from Persian exile to Judah, Nehemiah arrived safely in Jerusalem. Soon he conducted a personal inspection of the walls which had been destroyed during the Babylonian invasion of the sixth century B.C. A man of vision and initiative, he then committed himself to motivating the Jewish people to rebuild the walls.

Nehemiah quickly moved the people from motivation to action. He made specific work assignments, organized elaborate plans to frustrate the opponents of the building project, and led the people to complete the task in the amazingly short time of 52 days.

In a spirit of worship Nehemiah led the people to express their gratitude to God. The dedication of the completed walls included "songs of thanksgiving," "the music of cymbals, harps, and lyres," the use of "two large choirs to give thanks," "great sacrifices," and much "rejoicing" (Neh. 12:27,31,43, NIV).

An additional clue to the power of Nehemiah's leadership model for deacons lies in his reaction to the ways former governors and their assistants had "placed a heavy burden on the people" and "lorded it over the people" (Neh. 5:15, NIV). In sharp contrast, Nehemiah wrote that "out of reverence for God I did not act like that. Instead, I devoted myself to the work on this wall" (Neh. 5:15-16, NIV).

What makes a deacon an effective leader? Led by God, such a deacon chooses a participatory style of leadership. Nehemiah did more than coordinate the rebuilding of the walls; he helped build them. Deacons cannot simply sit back, plan projects, and call the shots; they must work alongside those who follow their guidance. Deacons may find it helpful to adopt what I call "a theology of chipping in."

7. *Effective deacons lead by staying with a task until they complete it, despite all obstacles.*—Succeeding Moses as the leader of the Israelites, Joshua received both an encouragement and a leadership assignment from God: "As I was with Moses, so I will be with you; I will never leave you or forsake you. Be strong and courageous, because you will lead these people to inherit the land I swore to their forefathers to give them" (Josh. 1:5-6, NIV).

Joshua's leadership in the conquest of Canaan required patience and perseverance. Obstacles thrived. For example, after the Israelites destroyed Jericho, Achan acted unfaithfully in stealing some of the holy things of the city, causing God to respond angrily against Israel (7:1). As a result, when Joshua sent about 3,000 men to capture Ai, they were defeated. When the Israelites disciplined Achan, God's favor returned to them (7:26).

Joshua then led the Israelites in battle after battle, defeating king after king. He helped the Israelites overcome the harshness of day-to-day military life by leading them to stay close to God. They built an altar to God, offered burnt offerings and fellowship offerings, listened to the reading of the book of the Law, and engaged in covenantal renewal (8:30-31,35).

A new menace emerged, however: worship of pagan gods. Joshua refused to yield. In his farewell address to the Israelites, he continued to take a stand: "As for me and my household, we will serve the Lord" (24:15, NIV). The people then vowed that they, too, would serve the Lord. Joshua concluded his remarkable life of leadership by making a covenant for the people at Shechem (24:25).

Joshua's life demonstrates for deacons how to stay with a task until they complete it. He committed himself to God's mission, communicated with God regularly, responded constructively to God's discipline when the people abandoned their assignment, refused to cave in to difficulties, led the people to worship in thanksgiving for victories, and engaged the people in covenantal relationship with God.

Imitation of Joshua's model can motivate deacons who stay close to their calling to claim with Paul: "I have fought the good fight, I have finished the race, I have kept the faith" (2 Tim. 4:7, NIV). What better legacy could any deacon leave to God and the church?

8. *Effective deacons lead by modeling a sacrificial spirit.*—The article on stewardship in *The Baptist Faith and Message* statement of Southern Baptists describes God as "the source of all blessings" and asserts that Christians live "under obligation to serve Him with their time, talents, and material possessions." To apply this obligation faithfully, deacons need to be willing to deny themselves and take up their crosses in following Christ as Lord. This approach to leadership makes an indelible mark on those ministered to by deacons.

The apostle Paul possessed an incredible willingness to sacrifice himself in order to lead out in the mission work of the early church. Persistent hostility greeted him in city after city. Consider the following illustrations from Acts:

● Victimized soon after his conversion by a plot of the Jews in Damascus to kill him, Paul escaped to Jerusalem (9:23-26).

● In Pisidia, Antioch Jews incited persecution against Paul and Barnabas, forcing their expulsion from the area (13:50).

● Some Jews came to Lystra from Antioch and Iconium and influenced the crowd to stone Paul and drag him outside the city, believing he was dead (14:19).

● In Philippi, in a series of dramatic developments, "The crowd joined in the attack against Paul and Silas, and the magistrates ordered them to be stripped and beaten. After they had been severely flogged, they were thrown into prison" (16:22-23, NIV).

● In Jerusalem a mob seized Paul, dragged him from the temple, and tried to kill him (21:30-31).

● Imprisoned on a ship sailing to Rome, Paul experienced a violent storm and a shipwreck off the coast of Malta (27:18,41).

● And Paul even commented on "a thorn in my flesh" (2 Cor. 12:7), but he moved quickly to say, "I will boast all the more gladly about my weaknesses, so that Christ's power may rest on me. That is why, for Christ's sake, I delight in weaknesses, in insults, in hardships, in persecutions, in difficulties. For when I am weak, then I am strong" (vv. 9-10, NIV).

Contemporary deacons willing to capture and live by that spirit can inject new meaning into their leadership role in church life.

Deacon Leadership is Practical

History can inform and inspire deacon leadership. Evidence follows. John Gurnsey, Baptist deacon in the town of Amenia, Dutchess County, New York, from the 1790s to the early 1840s, modeled biblical principles of leadership in key ways.[6]

Gurnsey modeled humility. Consistent in conduct and faithful to Christ, he was still willing to confess his sins. He claimed no superiority over others. And he was willing to perform any task, regardless of how lowly, in ministering to fellow church members and neighbors.

He also modeled a kind heart. Without neglecting his business, he made time to visit the sick, the poor, and the afflicted, whether they were church members or not. The following account shows how his inner compulsion to serve expressed itself in a concrete ministry of compassion:

> Once, when the winter was very severe and the snow deep, blocking up all the roads, he thought of a poor sister in the church, who lived about a mile from his residence, and could not rest without going to

see her; he was afraid she was in want. Though then an old man, he went with his staff in one hand, and a basket of provision in the other, and with much difficulty reached the house. The poor woman saw him coming, and her heart was deeply affected in witnessing his exertions to wade through the snow. He was a welcome visitor: she and her children were really in want; their fuel and provisions were all gone, or nearly so. He returned home wearied and exhausted, and immediately dispatched his team to take her some wood.[7]

Little did this faithful deacon know that his sacrificial effort would be recorded and would serve as a teaching device to help you understand what it means to develop a caring style of leadership.

Gurnsey modeled a generous approach to stewardship. His annual subscription for the pastor's support always exceeded anyone else's. He contributed liberally to missions. Even when he died, he left $1,000 to his church and $700-$800 each for home and foreign missions.

He modeled a faithful Christian witness. Besides leading his family in daily worship, he shared the gospel with people wherever he went. For 30 years he "sustained" a weekly prayer meeting in a schoolhouse in his neighborhood.

He modeled commitment to his church. He attended public worship regularly. He had a large covered wagon built so that he could take his family and friends to church. When the church erected a new house of worship and a parsonage, "the great burden of the care and labor fell upon him." He served as long as possible. The last time he distributed the elements of the Lord's Supper, he had to use crutches.

He modeled a cooperative spirit. He diligently promoted the welfare of other churches. He and his family attended revival meetings at churches miles from their home. Neighboring churches facing trouble often enlisted his prayers and help.

Gurnsey was not perfect. But his defects seemed minor compared to his spiritual strengths. Two comments of his biographer summarize the thrust of his life. First, "No hurry or press of business was allowed to direct him from his high and holy purpose to serve God." Second, "It was not because he had better gifts than others, that he was so much more useful, but because he was willing to use what he had."[8]

So goes the story of deacon John Gurnsey.

How does your story read? Perhaps the following self-testing instrument can help you decide. Simply answer yes, no, or sometimes to each statement. Then evaluate your responses on the basis of the biblical principles of leadership described in this chapter.

1. I try to live daily under the lordship of Christ.
2. I am committed to the historic purposes of the church.
3. I engage daily in personal devotions and family worship.
4. I respond enthusiastically to God's will for my life.
5. I seek to encourage, motivate, equip, and serve others.
6. I regularly assist other deacons in assessing ministries needing to be done, setting goals for achieving them, developing strategies, mobilizing resources, working cooperatively, and expressing thanksgiving to God for positive results.
7. I usually stay with a task until it is completed, despite all obstacles.
8. I possess a sacrificial spirit.

Robert Sheffield writes that deacons provide leadership in three ways: serving as an example to the church, participating in church life, and serving as catalyst leaders who help the church initiate activities to achieve its mission. He then suggests that each deacon group develop a Deacon Ministry Leadership Plan made up of projects to be done during the year. Suggested projects include fellowship enrichment, stewardship support, church organization support and involvement, the church understanding and practicing Baptist polity, interpreting the work of the church and the denomination, and involving church members in Pastoral Ministries program work.[9]

Consider ordering Sheffield's book. Urge your deacons to sponsor some of the projects identified in it. As your deacons model biblical principles of leadership, your church may begin to pulsate with a new sense of spiritual excitement. May the likes of Joel B. Lemon and John Gurnsey live on!

[1]Information about Joel Lemon comes from the article by Lynn C. Dickerson, II, "Joel B. Lemon, 1828-1910: Portrait of a Nineteenth-Century Baptist Deacon," *The Virginia Baptist Register* 25 (1986):1,275-85.

[2]From the Holy Bible, *New International Version,* copyright © 1973, 1978, 1984 by International Bible Society. Subsequent quotations are marked NIV.

[3]Robert Sheffield, *The Ministry of Baptist Deacons* (Nashville: Convention Press, 1990), 60-62. You may order this resource by calling toll-free 1-800-458-BSSB.

[4]*Minutes,* Old Colony Baptist Association (Massachusetts), October 1837, 11-13.

[5]Toby Druin, "Asheville," *Home Missions,* 46 (June-July 1975):29.

[6]Information about John Gurnsey comes from the section titled "Biographical," *The Baptist Memorial and Monthly Chronicle,* 1 (October 1842):299-303.

[7]Ibid., 300.

[8]Ibid., 301, 302.

[9]Sheffield, 62-69.

2
Deacons Leading in Church Ministry

Charles Warnock III

Charles Belt is a businessman living in Charlottesville, Virginia.

"Okay, now that we've decided to elect deacons," commented one of our young church leaders, "shouldn't we also decide what our deacons should do?"

The question was posed during the first meeting of our newly formed committee to formulate deacon policies. Our congregation was barely one year old, and we had grown to the point of needing to expand our leadership base. We were developing guidelines for deacon selection and ministry. But we hadn't come to that point easily.

When our church was founded, many of our own church leaders did not want to elect deacons right away. "Deacons ought to do something besides trying to run the church," came one comment. Another said, "I'm not sure what deacons ought to do, but I don't think I've ever seen a deacon group that did it." So we had waited.

But we had not waited idly. In our Discipleship Training sessions, we laid the groundwork for a better understanding of who deacons are and what they do. Our members studied the concept of spiritual gifts. They learned that different gifts were given to various persons in order for the church to function as the body of

Christ. In the case of deacons specifically, our members drew some conclusions about what our soon-to-be-elected deacons ought to be and do. Our deacons, we decided, would be "ministry encouragers" to the congregation.

A New Testament Model

If our deacons were going to encourage ministry, we needed to observe some models of effective deacon ministry. But where would we find one?

One committee member suggested we contact other churches with outstanding deacon ministry programs. We could ask them what their deacons did and model our program from theirs. We took note of that suggestion for future reference.

Another suggested we gather all the published deacon ministry material we could. We would study those books and pamphlets for guidance. Another good suggestion, we thought, but still we weren't satisfied.

Finally, one member of our committee asked, "Why don't we look at the New Testament examples of deacon ministry first?" Our congregation had made a previous commitment to biblically based ministry. The suggestion to use the New Testament models was so obvious we had almost overlooked it.

The traditional deacon passages in 1 Timothy 3 and Titus interested our members. But those passages seemed to focus more on what deacons ought to *be* than on what they should *do*. And, our church recently had adopted deacon qualifications based on those passages. Our members now were searching for models of deacon ministry. Or as one member put it, "We need examples of deacons who deak!"

Of all the New Testament passages we studied, we settled on Acts 6:1-7 as our model for deacon ministry. In a careful study of the passage, I pointed out that the seven mentioned in Acts 6 probably were the forerunners of those who later would officially be called deacons. Our members understood that we did not have to duplicate everything in the Acts 6 passage. We did see that account as a valid model for effective deacon ministry, however.

In Acts 6:1-7, a problem had arisen in the fellowship of the Jerusalem church. The controversy divided the congregation along ethnic lines. The Jews of Greek descent complained that the Aramaic-speaking Jews were neglecting Greek widows in the daily food distribution. Obviously, the congregation's attempt to minister to the widows had been well-intentioned. But for some reason, the Greek-speaking members felt their widows were being slighted. Ministry, in either the New Testament period or now, isn't always as successful as we would like it to be. So the early church leaders were faced with solving a ministry problem. How would they deal with this problem, encourage ministry in others, and stay true to their calling?

Quickly the twelve decided that they couldn't do everything. They concluded that " 'it would not be right for us to neglect the ministry of the word of God in order to wait on tables.' " (Acts 6:2, NIV)[1]

The twelve suggested that others be chosen from the congregation to encourage effective ministry. The congregation was instructed to " 'choose seven men from among you who are known to be full of the Spirit and wisdom.' " (Acts 6:3, NIV) The twelve would then turn the ministry of caring for widows over to the chosen seven.

According to Luke's account, the suggestion pleased the entire congregation. That was a miracle in itself! Seven men were chosen by the congregation and set apart for this special ministry by the twelve.

Acts 6:7 tells the rest of the story. "So the word of God spread. The number of disciples in Jerusalem increased rapidly, and a large number of priests became obedient to the faith" (Acts 6:7, NIV). These seven set the standard for effective deacon ministry. Not only did they solve the problem of the distribution of food, they helped the church get back to its main task of proclaiming the gospel effectively!

Several lessons can be learned from the Acts 6 passage. First, even the most well-intentioned ministry can encounter problems. It was true of the Jerusalem congregation and todays' congregations. Second, the pastor and staff cannot solve every ministry problem, and they shouldn't have to! Third, God has placed spiritually mature members in every congregation, just as He had in the Jerusalem congregation. Fourth, when set aside to the task, these mature leaders (we call them "deacons") can solve the problems of ministry and help keep the church true to its mission of telling the good news.

Personal Qualities that Encourage

Finding a biblical role model for our deacon ministry is challenging. But now that we have the Acts 6 model, how can we translate that account into the life of 20th-century congregations? It's important to communicate the idea that deacons are responsible for encouraging their church in all aspects of ministry.

How can we define ministry? Ministry is anything we do to fulfill God's purpose for His church. Worship, Sunday School, Discipleship Training, missions organizations, outreach, fellowship, and special projects are ways to do ministry. And deacons need to be "front and center" leaders, both doing and encouraging others in all these areas.

While some churches opt to spell out specific deacon ministry requirements, I prefer a more general approach. Deacons should support the ministries of the church through prayer, attitude, attendance, and stewardship.

Prayer

Prayer is a primary means of encouraging church ministries. Deacons should spend a great deal of their meeting time praying for the needs and ministries of their congregation. Church members frequently communicate prayer requests to deacons through the Deacon Family Ministry Plan. A deacon-led prayer chain can respond quickly to urgent prayer needs. Personally, deacons should be encouraged to develop and devote private time to prayer for their church. Church members are encouraged when they know that deacons pray.

Positive Attitude

As a pastor, my experiences with deacons have been overwhelmingly positive. Those previous deacon groups I have worked with exhibited positive attitudes toward their church and its ministries.

Deacons ought to exhibit positive attitudes because they are models for other church members. Deacons who have a basic belief in the integrity and effectiveness of their church can be a great encouragement to less mature members. But having a positive attitude toward the church does not mean that deacons ignore problems that arise in the fellowship.

The twelve in Acts 6 faced the problem in their congregation head-on. Rather than denying the problem, they suggested a positive solution to it. Deacons have the same responsibility today.

Problems are a product of working with people. Misunderstandings, hurt feelings, honest differences of opinion, and mistakes can create difficulty within any congregation. The responsibility of deacons is to face the problem positively, not deny it.

Deacons can exhibit a positive attitude in several ways. First, deacons can communicate with the congregation regularly. Members can constantly be reminded, "If you have questions about anything in our church life, please feel free to ask your deacon."

Second, deacons can acknowledge problems when they exist. One experience in my church illustrates this point. We were unable to provide printed financial statements to our congregation for over four months. We had made the mistake of moving into our first building and changing computer accounting programs at the same time. Although we could provide our members with bank balances and a general financial picture, specific budget account figures were not available for four months.

Some members became understandably concerned. Some thought we didn't know our financial condition. Others speculated that money from the building fund was being used for other purposes. Some wondered why it was so difficult to get a printed report "because we've always had one." Members called their deacons and asked pointed questions about the church's finances.

Fortunately, our deacons were informed and faced the problem honestly and positively. Our deacon chairman gave the congregation as much information as we could gather. His assurance that our financial house was in order calmed many fears. His promise that financial reports would be available when the new accounting software was loaded reassured our members. Through it all, the positive attitude of our deacons in a negative situation made the difference.

Regular Attendance
Deacons should support the church with their attendance although this does not necessarily mean "every time the doors are open." Because deacons are involved in different ministries and have different schedules, not all deacons are expected to attend every church meeting.

Deacons are expected, however, to encourage others to attend church by attending themselves. A deacon cannot honestly invite someone to Sunday School, worship, or Discipleship Training if that deacon doesn't attend himself. Deacons are leaders. Leaders lead by example as well as exhortation. Deacons who tell church members what they ought to do but don't do it themselves are not effective encouragers.

Deacons should attend church worship and study opportunities because they desire to grow spiritually and to encourage others to do the same. Deacons should take seriously their need to lead through attendance, and others follow their example.

Stewardship
When deacon ministry is based on Acts 6, some questions are easier to answer than others. Should deacons lead the congregation through prayer? Of course. Should deacons exhibit a positive, problem-solving attitude? Again, the answer is yes. Should deacons support the ministries of the church with their attendance? Yes, again. One difficult question remains, however.

How should deacons lead through stewardship? Some churches think that deacons should be required to tithe. Others think that real stewardship doesn't stop with the tithe. Some people believe that giving is a private matter between the giver and God. One thing most people agree on is that deacons should encourage other church members by being good stewards themselves.

After a great deal of discussion, my congregation adopted the statement that deacons should "demonstrate a biblical commitment to stewardship." We believed that if we chose persons who were "full of the Spirit and wisdom," stewardship of possessions would be a part of their spiritual maturity. Persons charged with the task of encouraging the church in ministry ought to make a significant commitment to the programs and principles of that ministry.

Actions that Encourage

Deacons ought to be on the frontline of encouraging ministry. Deacons, however, are busy people. The demands of family, work, civic, and church activities can quickly fill up a calendar. The deacons at my church have said, "We want to be busy deacons, but we want to be effective, too." Effectiveness to them meant projects that encouraged others to minister, too.

Over the years we tried different approaches to deacons encouraging church ministries. Quite honestly, some were more successful than others. After each attempt, we evaluated the project and its effectiveness. We learned from our failures and successes. Here are 10 deacon actions we took which seemed to encourage our congregation in ministry. They are not exhaustive nor normative for all Southern Baptist churches. Hopefully, they will generate ideas for deacon ministry that you may want to consider for your church.

A Deacon-Led Prayer Ministry

Deacons don't always have to initiate a project in order to lead in it. Our deacon-led prayer ministry began because several members of our congregation requested it. Our deacons took the request and implemented a church-wide prayer ministry that is still continuing.

The prayer ministry began as a prayer request letter. Our congregation met in rented space for the first three years of our existence. Because the space was only available on Sunday, we did not have a combined midweek prayer service. Many of our members missed the opportunity to share prayer requests with the entire church body. They asked that the deacons lead a churchwide prayer ministry.

A prayer request letter was begun. Members could leave their requests on Sunday during the morning worship service, or they could call their deacon with their request. The deacon would then relay the prayer requests to the church staff. Requests would then be included in that week's prayer letter.

The weekly prayer request letter arrived in our members' homes about midweek. We punched the letter to fit a three-ring notebook and encouraged members to file their letters each week. Deacons and staff members would follow up on the requests and include answers to specific requests in the following weeks' letters.

Once we moved into our own church building, we no longer needed the prayer request letter. Our deacons suggested that we adopt a deacon-led prayer chain. Each deacon called his assigned families to ask if they would like to be included in the prayer chain. Only urgent requests would be channeled through the prayer chain. Regular requests were included in our weekly church newsletter.

When a deacon learns of an urgent request for prayer, he immediately calls the deacon chairman. The chairman then contacts each of the other 11 deacons. Those deacons then call their assigned prayer chain families. Breaking the prayer chain into 12 small "chains," instead of one long one, shortens the time for calling. It also keeps the chain from being broken if the next person on the list is not available.

The prayer chain has worked effectively for our congregation. It gives the deacons an opportunity to encourage their families to pray for specific requests. Our church members also get to see our deacons actually doing ministry.

Deacon Telephone Contacts

One of the first things our newly-elected deacons said to me as pastor was, "We don't mind calling our members, but please give us a reason to call." Since their request, deacon telephone contacts have been designed to be specific and purposeful.

Rather than just telling our deacons, "Please call your families," we now give specific reasons for them to call. When we began designing our first church building, our deacons called all their families. Deacons asked members for design suggestions and talked to them about the scope of the project. Our members had a chance to ask their deacons questions about the building and to volunteer to serve on various building committees.

Deacons then returned to the next deacons meeting with questions, concerns, and ideas. Many of the design suggestions were eventually incorporated into our building plans.

Our deacons also have called to invite families to special events, to inform them of significant business sessions, to poll them about their opinion on various issues facing our church, and to ask for their prayer support. Giving our deacons a specific reason to call encourages our members to continue to be involved in church ministries.

Deacon Adopt-a-Prospect Plan

Not only do our deacons have responsibility for specific church member families through the Deacon Family Ministry Plan, they also "adopt" prospect families, too. Prospect families are assigned to a deacon just like member families are. Our deacons call these prospect families to thank them for worshiping with us and to encourage them to participate in other activities.

Prospects are also invited to attend special programs like our Deacon Family Ministry Banquet, Valentine Banquet, and other churchwide activities. This deacon "adopt-a-prospect" program gives the prospective family an early relationship with our deacons. Some of our prospects have commented on how many different people contacted them during their "get-acquainted days" at our church. This deacon involvement in outreach also encourages others to be involved in outreach as well.

Deacon Family Ministry Plan

Our deacons use the Deacon Family Ministry Plan as the framework for their ministry to our congregation. Before we adopted the plan, we discussed other methods of deacon ministry. We concluded that the Deacon Family Ministry Plan served our purposes better than anything else we could think of.

Here's how our Deacon Family Ministry Plan works: Our deacons are assigned eight to twelve families each. Each deacon is responsible for making contact with his assigned families and getting to know them personally. As new member and prospect families are added, these are distributed evenly among the deacons. As I mentioned earlier, after the initial contact, we give our deacons specific reasons to contact their families.

We assign families to our deacons by taking into account specific family characteristics including age range, area in which they live, or expressed interest in some special aspect of our church's life. Our deacon family assignments are purposely not the same as their Sunday School class or other church group. We want our deacon ministry to cut across other organization lines. This gives us another way of making contact with our families.

For more information on the Deacon Family Ministry Plan, order the *Deacon Family Ministry Plan Resource Book* from your LifeWay Christian Store or by calling 1-800-458-2772.

Deacon Sponsored Special Events

Our deacons host an annual "Deacon Family Ministry Banquet." The banquet has two purposes. First, each deacon introduces all his new member families since the previous year. Second, deacons invite prospect families for which they are responsible, to give them a look at our church family.

The banquet is organized differently from our other church events, too. Although the entire church is invited, it's really like 12 mini-banquets going on in the same room. Each deacon is responsible for inviting all the families assigned to him, both member and prospect. Each deacon is also responsible for planning the menu for his deacon families. He asks them to bring certain items and invites them to sit at the same table with him and his family.

When we first discussed this idea, we weren't sure it would work. What if some deacon's families didn't come? What if a deacon didn't have enough food for his group? Would families respond if they had to bring food to share with eight to ten other families? We decided that the possible fellowship gains were worth the risks, however. When the evening for the banquet came, we were surprised and delighted. Our first Deacon Family Ministry Banquet produced the highest attendance our young congregation had ever had for a fellowship event! Each deacon hosted his families. Food was spread family-style at each deacon's assigned tables. No one had to wait in a long buffet line, and the get-acquainted conversation produced new friendships within our church.

Our deacons have also hosted ice cream fellowships, picnics, and barbecues. These fellowship events provide informal opportunities for deacons and families to get to know each other in a comfortable atmosphere.

Special Deacon-Led Projects
Our deacons believe that they have a responsibility to encourage others to minister in special ways. When a widow in our congregation needed her house painted, our deacons took on the task of getting it done. Work groups were organized, painting equipment rounded up, and several painting days were scheduled.

Even when the project took longer than anticipated, the deacon in charge kept at it. More paint was purchased. Deacons called their families and enlisted more "painters." Eventually, the job was finished. Although it took longer than we had planned, the church was encouraged by the perseverance and example of our deacons who were personally involved in doing something for someone else.

Deacon New-Member Involvement

Involvement with new members begins immediately with our deacons. The deacon has been assigned the new family before they join. The deacon has contacted the prospective member family on several occasions, possibly to invite them to a churchwide event.

But deacon new-member involvement also includes Deacon Family Ministry Plan responsibilities. Deacons visit again in the homes of families after they join. As in many churches our deacons present the new members' packet and gather additional information about the family. They also answer any questions the family may still have about our church.

Our deacons are also involved in new-member orientation. One of our deacons leads this four-week new-member introduction that we call the "Discovery Class." During this class deacons take the lead in explaining the various ministries in our church. These deacons also encourage the newest members to find God's place of service for them.

Both the Christian Service Survey and a spiritual gifts inventory are given to our new members. Deacons pick up these ministry-interest indicators on follow-up home visits. Both through word and action deacons encourage our new members to get involved in the ministries that God has chosen for them.

Deacon-Led Worship Experiences

One of the strongest memories I have of growing up in a Southern Baptist church is a deacon memory. I can still see the deacons at the Eastern Heights Baptist Church filing in to sit on the front row just before the morning worship service began. Their faithfulness and commitment impressed me as a junior boy. Few churches hold to the tradition of deacons filling the front pew, but deacons still should be leaders in worship.

Our deacons are given opportunities to lead in portions of the worship service each week. A ministry-oriented prayer time is reserved for a different deacon at each service. We believe that our members need to see our deacons leading in worship for several reasons. First, if members see deacons regularly involved in the service, they know that deacons are present. Second, when deacons led in worship, our members know that worship is not just the domain of the pastor or staff.

Deacons are called upon at appropriate services to read Scripture, give testimonies, present the children's sermon, and sing. Often our deacon officers are asked to make important announcements to the congregation. This deacon involvement creates a sense of participation and ownership in all that we do, including worship.

Deacons also administer the Lord's Supper and assist with baptism. Although these are typical deacon-led duties in many Southern Baptist churches, they are still occasions for deacons to encourage others as they lead in worship.

Deacon Committee and Church Leadership Team Involvement

Our deacons do not call themselves a "board." Nor do they pretend that they "run" the church. But our deacons do lead our congregation administratively as they serve on various committees and the Church Leadership Team.

Unlike some churches we do not require that a deacon be on every committee. But because our congregation has charged our deacons with "guarding the fellowship of the church," many of our deacons do serve on administrative committees. The chairman of deacons is also a member of the Church Leadership Team.

Through their faithful service on various committees, our deacons engage in positive problem-solving, participate with other members in planning, and demonstrate their own commitment to our congregation. Other members are encouraged to accept positions of ministry responsibility by the example of our deacons.

Deacon Church Program Involvement

I heard of a church that would not allow its deacons to do anything except hold the office of deacon. They wanted the best they could get from their deacons and felt that a deacon's energy and time would be diluted by other church involvement. While I sympathize with this church, I disagree with their decision.

First, in our young congregation we could not afford for our deacons to have only one responsibility. Many of our best Sunday School teachers, department directors, Discipleship Training leaders, and mission advocates are deacons. Second, and more importantly, we do not see deacon ministry in conflict with church programs. We see deacon ministry as a complement to other church programs.

As I mentioned earlier, we expect our deacons to be at church. Attendance is not optional for deacons. But more than that, we ask our deacons to take church program responsibilities appropriate to their gifts and calling. Deacons teach Sunday School, sing in the choir, participate in mission projects, lead discipleship groups, coach softball teams, and recruit others to do the same.

Sometimes deacon ministry duties overlap. Some deacons teach adults for whom they also have family ministry responsibilities. Most of the time, however, these other ministry duties reflect the desire of our deacons to encourage others in these same church programs.

As a pastor, I am thankful for that committee member who asked the question, "Shouldn't we decide what we want our deacons to do?"

His question started us on a long, rewarding journey. We searched Scripture for deacon ministry models. We prayed for God's guidance as we formulated deacon policies. We agonized over deacon qualifications. We listened to the disappointments of deacon ministries that failed and dreamed together of a deacon ministry that would succeed. And most of all, we found that deacons can be the best encouragers for ministry that a church could have!

---

[1]From the Holy Bible, *New International Version,* copyright © 1973, 1978, 1984 by International Bible Society. Subsequent quotations are marked NIV.

3
Deacons Leading in Community Ministry

Gary Hardin

Gary Hardin is Pastor, Packard Road Baptist Church, Ann Arbor, Michigan.

O n Friday evening, after arriving home from work, Bob Lancaster took off his suit and tie. He would need to wear comfortable clothing on this night. He eyed the various articles of clothing in his closet and chose jeans, a sport shirt, and a pair of comfortable shoes. After eating a light snack, Bob headed for the church. Bob's church participated in Room in the Inn, a community-wide project for assisting homeless persons. Bob, and several other deacons, had volunteered to help with this ministry.

The aroma from the church's kitchen let Bob know that a delicious meal was being prepared for the dozen homeless men, women, and children who would be sleeping at the church on this Friday night. Other churches in town also participated in the Room in the Inn ministry. This project, sponsored jointly by three social agencies and local churches, provided homeless individuals with friendship, food, and warm places to sleep on cold nights.

At 6:30 p.m. a van arrived on the church parking lot. Bob and other members from the church greeted their guests and ushered them to the church kitchen. After enjoying the hot meal, several of the men and women sat around the tables and drank a second cup of coffee and talked while the children played board games.

By 8:30 p.m. cots and blankets had been set up in several class-rooms. The children were put to bed early. They would need a night of rest in a warm building.

Bob and several members of his church would stay all night and host these special guests. The hosts would listen as the guests shared about the circumstances of their lives that had led to their homelessness. By 10:30 p.m. everyone was sound asleep.

At 7:30 a.m. on Saturday morning, breakfast was being served. The dozen "guests" expressed their thanks to Bob and other members of his church for their hospitality and friendship. At 8:30 a.m. the van that had delivered the guests had arrived on the church's parking lot to take the guests back to places of their choosing.

Inside the church building, Bob and his fellow church members cleaned dishes and put chairs and tables back into the Sunday School rooms which had been converted into makeshift bedrooms for the homeless persons.

Mixed emotions troubled Bob. Watching the van drive away had left Bob feeling sad and helpless. On the other hand, Bob did feel good about himself. He and other members of his church had brought a few happy hours into the lives of a dozen seemingly hopeless people.

The Deacon: A Minister-Leader in the Community

The Christian life has been described as having a *vertical relationship* (a relationship and ministry to God) and a *horizontal relationship* (a relationship and ministry to other people). The vertical relationship might be called "the inward journey" (toward God), while the horizontal relationship might be viewed as "the outward journey" (toward the world).

Your service as a deacon minister needs both of these focuses. Your church provides a context for you to make progress in both the inward and outward journey. As you participate in Deacon Family Ministry Plan, serve on a committee, witness, teach a class, or sing in a choir, you grow in your relationships with God and with other people.

Your community provides you with a second context in which to make progress in the inward and outward journey. Participation in civic clubs, lending a hand in community projects, and involvement in political issues are ways you can express the inward and outward dimension of your deacon ministry and your Christian faith.

Jesus expressed the inward and outward dimensions of His ministry *inside* the temple and synagogues. Jesus devoted portions of His ministry to activities connected with the temple and synagogues. He read Old Testament Scripture while attending a service at a synagogue (Luke 4:16). Jesus and His disciples participated in synagogue activities (John 6:59). Jesus taught in the temple (John 18:20).

But Jesus also practiced the inward and outward dimensions of His ministry *outside* the temple and synagogues. He healed a begging blind man who was seated by the road (Mark 10:46-52). As Jesus walked beside the Sea of Galilee, He invited two fishermen to become disciples (Mark 1:16). While standing in a cornfield, Jesus taught important principles about the Sabbath Day (Luke 6:1-5).

Your servant ministry needs to be expressed toward people *in* the church, but it also needs to be expressed toward people *outside* the church, namely the community. Deacons serve as Christ's ministers both to the church and to the community. Church-centered deacon ministry helps build up the body of Christ. Community-centered deacon ministry helps build up the body of Christ, too.

Community Leadership: A Biblical Perspective

Deacons know they are servants and leaders in their churches. What many deacons never have considered is that they can be servants and leaders in their communities, as well. *What does it mean to be a leader in my community?* you might be thinking. Three Bible texts help define community leadership. That is, three Bible passages shed some light on ways deacons, and all believers, can provide Christian leadership in their communities.

Be a Christian Influence in the Community (Matt. 5:13)

Jesus said to His disciples, "Ye are the salt of the earth." The primary use of salt is to season food. Baked potatoes or scrambled eggs with no salt sprinkled on them have a bland taste. Jesus' analogy about being the salt of the earth reminded His followers that they could help season or influence their communities for the better.

When deacons seek to be the "salt of the earth," they provide community leadership. As deacons live exemplary life-styles and practice Christian teachings in their communities, those communities are made better. Never underestimate the power of your Christian life-style to season or influence your community. Can you imagine what the moral quality of your community would be if there was no Christian influence?

Delos Miles, a seminary professor, toured the USS Nicholas when it was being commissioned. While on board the ship, Miles met a chief petty officer who had served in the Navy for almost 40 years. The officer said, "I am not *in* the Navy. I *am* the Navy.[1] As a deacon, you are not just *in* a serving-leading role. You *are* a servant-leader. And as you seek to be an influence for Jesus Christ in your community, you help build bridges of evangelism between your church and the people of your community.

Do Good Works in the Community (Matt. 5:14-16)

Jesus said of Himself, "I am the light of the world" (John 8:12). When Jesus declared that His followers were "the light of the world" (Matt. 5:14-16), He demanded nothing less than that they should be like Him. Light is meant to be seen. People don't light candles and then place those lighted candles under earthen bushel measures. Therefore, said Jesus, "Let your light so shine before men, that they may see your good works, and glorify your Father which is in heaven" (Matt. 5:16).

The word *good* in this verse is packed with meaning. Two Greek words were often translated "good." The first word meant a thing was good in its quality. The second word meant not just good in quality but also attractive, alluring, magnetic, charming. The second Greek word is the one used in Matthew 5:16.[2]

When deacons faithfully practice good works in their communities, other people are attracted by, drawn by, those good works to find what their source is. The result is that those searching people discover the source of deacons' good works—the deacons' lives have been changed positively through their faith in Jesus Christ. Deacons practice good works because they want to be like Jesus, of whom it was said, He "went about doing good" (Acts 10:38).

Form a Partnership with Fellow Believers (Phil. 1:1-5)

In addressing pastors and deacons at Philippi, Paul expressed his gratitude for their "fellowship" (a word meaning partnership) in the gospel (v. 5). Paul knew the powerful, life-changing work of the gospel was not carried out most effectively by one person but by all believers as they joined hands to serve Christ together.

A deacon can provide clothes for needy people. But think how much more clothing could be given if several congregations participated in such a project. One deacon can do his part to help eliminate poverty in the community. But wouldn't that effort be more effective if a group of deacons or deacons from several churches took part?

Whenever your church has an opportunity to join with other churches to address community issues, encourage your church to participate. Become an advocate for associational ministries that seek to meet needs in your community. Urge your congregation to be involved in community action projects in which churches can participate.

A second-grade Sunday School teacher asked: "Johnny, what is your favorite parable?" Johnny replied, "The one where somebody loafs and fishes."[3]

Too many people loaf when there is work to be done. Community organizations need volunteers. Nursing home residents need visits. Elderly persons need their lawns mowed. Prisoners need encouragement. Poor people need food and clothing. Committed deacons, and their churches, can help meet some of these community needs through their influence, their good works, and their partnership with one another.

Don't lose sight of the reason churches and deacons must be involved in meeting community needs. The motive is not just to do good. Many unsaved people do good things. Social agencies do good work. Jesus pointed us to the motive for community involvement when he said of our visible good works: "That they may see your good works, and glorify your Father which is in Heaven" (Matt. 5:16). The motive for community involvement is to help build bridges of relationships among unsaved people, the Lord Jesus, and our churches. Deacons must practice community involvement from a distinctively Christian and evangelistic perspective.

The Changing Scene of America's Communities

Carlton Myers, a retired pastor, wrote a book titled, *It's Your Life, Enjoy It!*[4] The last chapter in the book had an interesting title: "Ready for Any Eventuality." That phrase, ready for any eventuality, provides a guide for deacons who wish to serve as community leaders. Be prepared for the possibility of almost anything because today's community life is drastically different from community life of 20, 30, or 40 years ago.

Today's Communities are More Urban

Today, fewer people than ever before live on farms or in rural areas. In fact, many areas that have been rural for years and years are becoming more urban. Small shopping centers are being built in once rural areas. Famous-name discount stores are opening businesses in communities that used to contain only farms. A tract of land that grew cotton, corn, or beans five years ago now has townhouses on it. Urbanization sometimes brings a faster pace of life, more stress, and changes in values and life-styles.

Today's Communities are Experiencing Population Changes

Urbanization usually brings new people to a community. The new people might not adhere to the traditional values of the folk who have lived in the community all their lives.

Communities across America today are not made up of people from the same ethnic origin. In some small towns and communities, medical service is provided almost entirely by Asian doctors. Is there a community anywhere in America today that does not have living in it people who are of different ethnic origins?

Today's Communities are Witnessing the Continued Breakdown of Family Life

We could only wish it was possible to move to a community where there was no divorce, no child abuse, no teenage pregnancies, or no alcohol problems in families. Such a place does not exist! All communities are being influenced by family breakdown. Estimates are that by the year 2,000 more than 50 percent of all children will live in single-parent homes.

Today's Communities are Made up of Diverse People

Pluralism is the term used to describe life in American communities today. This term reflects the diversity of people and life-styles in today's communities. On the same street may live a Japanese family, a black family, a man and woman who live together though not married, a single parent, a drug addict, a homosexual, a blue-collar worker, and a white-collar worker. On the same street may live a Southern Baptist family, a Buddhist family, a Jewish family, and a Mormon family.

The changing scene of America's communities presents us with these challenges and ministry opportunities:

• Urbanization has brought to some communities unemployment, higher crime rates, and increased usage of drugs and alcohol.

• Today's community residents are stressed and lonely. Many have no connection with a person or group who can provide emotional and spiritual support.

• Racial prejudice continues to plague many communities. The influx of people from different ethnic origins has caused some people to react with prejudice and hatred.

• Increased population in a community brings a demand for

more medical and human services and housing. In some communities these needs never really are met adequately.

● The gap between the haves and the have-nots is widening in many communities. Thus, there is more poverty and hunger in today's communities.

● Because of family breakdown in our communities, churches are having to minister to people who are trying to cope with great stress and emotional problems.

A man was walking on the beach early one morning. He noticed someone walking up ahead of him. The man watched as the person ahead picked up objects off the beach and threw them back into the water. The man began to walk faster until he caught up with the person ahead of him. The man discovered the person ahead of him was a teenage boy. The boy was picking up starfish left by the tide and was throwing the starfish back into the water.

"What are you doing?" the man asked. "I'm throwing these starfish back into the water. If they stay here on the beach, the sun will shine on them, and they will die."

"Young man, this beach goes on for many miles. There could be thousands, maybe millions of starfish lying on this beach. What difference do you think you can make?"

The boy looked at the starfish he was holding in his hand. Then he threw the starfish back into the water and said, "Well, all I know is that it makes a difference to this one starfish."[5]

Your church will not be able to meet all the needs of the people who live in your community. Don't let that concern prevent your church from becoming a ministering church. Your church's loving care and ministry can bring hope to one person and then to another.

The needs in today's communities are so severe and varied that churches cannot become preoccupied only with the events and activities that take place within church buildings. Churches must become more caring, more sensitive, and more patient with the diverse people who live in America's communities. The extent to which a church ministers to the community often depends on the quality of leadership given by the church's deacons.

The Deacon's Role in Community Leadership

Offer Your Acceptance to People
Once you begin to minister to your larger community you will encounter people who do not live by the Christian values that guide your life. Don't allow this tension to turn you off and to prevent you from wanting to associate with such people. *Acceptance* means we offer our love, friendship, and compassion to others without requiring them to meet our standards. By taking this approach to human relationships, we many times win the friendship of people, which in turn, opens the door for us to share about our faith and about the values that guide our lives.

Live an Exemplary Life Before People
If you live in a small town or community, you probably could drive down Main Street and make a list of business persons, shop owners, professional people, and civic leaders who do not attend any church. You know these people. They, in turn, probably know you. They know you are a deacon at _____ Baptist Church. The way you live your life before these people may determine whether they ever attend your church.

Become Personally Involved in your Community
Volunteer sometime to assist a social agency in your town. Join a civic club. Participate in political campaigns. Serve as a volunteer chaplain. Participate in school functions. Cooperate with your local Baptist association when it conducts community missions projects.

Link Needy Persons with Community Resources
Prepare a listing of all social agencies in your community and the services they provide. Include addresses and phone numbers. Find out the eligibility requirements for each agency. After having discovered this information you are prepared to link needy people with community resources. Make duplicate copies of this listing for other deacons and members of the congregation to use.

Guide the Church to Develop Benevolence Policies and Procedures

If a transient shows up at your church's office and asks for money, what will your church do? If a needy person phones the church and asks for food, how much assistance can your church give? These situations are only two examples that show your church needs benevolence policies and procedures. Chapter 5 of *The Ministry of Baptist Deacons* gives excellent advice for developing benevolence policies and procedures.[6]

Educate your Church About the Community

Do members of your congregation really know the makeup of the community? Are they aware of community problems? Do they realize the changes that are taking place in the community?

The deacons, working with the pastor, may wish to invite community leaders to talk to your congregation about community changes, community issues, and community concerns.

As a Deacon Leadership Project, the deacons could establish a Community Information Center in a high-traffic area of the church's buildings. A display could be set up that contains pamphlets, brochures, and other printed information about the community and help offered by community agencies. If you set up a Community Information Center, someone needs to be assigned the responsibility of keeping the information current.

Encourage the Church Council to assess community needs by using the *Church and Community Diagnosis Workbook.*[7]

Educate your Community About your Church

If your church has a public relations committee, this group can inform the community about the ministry of your church. If your church does not have such a committee, this might be a project the deacons could perform. Print a brochure about your church and its ministries. Brochures can be distributed to prospects during visitation emphases.

Consider advertising your church in the local newspaper. For maximum impact place the ads in a section other than the religious section of the paper. This request will cost more, but, in the long run, will be more effective.

If your church has available money, television and radio spots can be used to advertise special events your church is sponsoring. Billboards remind people of your church and its location.

Whenever your church participates in missions projects, community service projects, or sponsors special events, ask the local newspaper to give you some coverage. Many newspapers want such news and will be glad to provide the coverage.

Guide your Church to Develop Community Ministries

Work with appropriate committees, the pastor, and staff. The following section provides ideas for possible community ministries.

Community Leadership-Ministry Projects

Hundreds of ideas could be included in this section. What follows are only a few suggestions for worthy community leadership-ministry projects.

Hunger

- Establish a food bank at your church.
- Encourage your church to participate in community food bank projects.
- Observe World Hunger Day, a denominational emphasis.
- Take up a hunger offering periodically. Use the money to help feed the hungry.

Refugees and Homeless

- Adopt a refugee or homeless family. Provide necessary assistance to help this family become self-supporting.
- Participate in community projects to assist refugees and/or homeless persons.
- Encourage associational ministries to the homeless.
- Become an advocate for legislation that assists the homeless.
- Volunteer to work at a shelter.

Race Relations
- Observe Race Relations Sunday, a denominational emphasis.
- At regular intervals, ask a black or ethnic congregation to worship with your church.
- Teach the church biblical admonitions about love and acceptance of all people.

Pornography
- Become an advocate for legislation that will help stamp out pornography.
- Distribute printed materials that detail the evils and harmful effects of pornography.

Disaster Ministry
- Guide the church to develop a disaster action plan. This plan would outline steps the church would take to offer assistance in the event of a public disaster.
- Strengthen the church's Brotherhood and encourage participants in this program to provide disaster ministry.

Multiethnic Ministry
- Establish an ethnic Bible study, mission, or Sunday School class within the church.
- Teach English skills to ethnics.
- Provide job assistance, shelter, food, clothing, and medical services to needy persons.

Mentally Retarded
- Organize a Sunday School class for mentally retarded persons.
- Visit mentally retarded persons in their homes.
- Support the work of agencies that provide assistance for mentally retarded persons.
- Provide personal encouragement to church families with mentally retarded persons.

Elderly
- Establish a telephone chain to check daily on the well-being of elderly people in the church and/or community.
- Visit nursing home residents.
- Provide small appliance repair services for the elderly.

- Help the elderly with transportation needs.
- Perform yard work for elderly persons.

Troubled Youth
- Provide prenatal medical care for unwed teenage mothers.
- Participate in foster home ministries.
- Help troubled youth with job assistance.
- Become a friend to troubled youth.

Parents
- Guide the church to begin weekday education ministries such as day care and Mother's Day Out.
- Conduct parenting conferences and seminars.
- Have a Family Life Conference.

Prisoners
- Visit inmates.
- Minister to the families of inmates.
- Work with chaplains of jails and prisons to discover possible ministry projects with prisoners.
- Participate in religious services at a jail or prison.

Alcohol
- Minister and witness to persons with alcohol problems.
- Provide personal support and encouragement to families troubled by alcohol.
- Educate the church about the harmful effects of alcohol.
- The church could offer its facilities for Alcoholics Anonymous meetings.

Am I My Brother's Keeper?

After Cain murdered his brother, Abel, God confronted Cain about his misdeed (see Gen. 4:1-16). Cain raised a thoughtful question: *"Am I my brother's keeper?"* Of course, Cain asked this question to escape his personal accountability for murdering his brother.

The question, Am I my brother's keeper?, still remains for deacons and other Christians today. Many believers adopt an isolationist stance. This stance removes them from contact with non-Christians. This position also distances them from grappling with some of the pressing social and community problems of our day.

As followers of Christ we are our brother's keeper in the sense that we have a responsibility to minister to people in need. We are accountable for the witness we give or do not give. We do have an obligation to use our personal resources and gifts for the betterment of people. '

[1]Thom S. Rainer, ed., *Evangelism in the Twenty-First Century* (Wheaton, Illinois: Harold Shaw Publishers, 1989), 58.

[2]William Barclay, *The Gospel of Matthew,* Vol. 1 in *The Daily Study Bible* (Philadelphia: Westminster Press, 1958), 121.

[3]Bob C. Hardison, *Happiness Is No Secret* (Nashville: Broadman Press, 1987), 82.

[4]Carlton Myers, *It's Your Life, Enjoy It!* (Nashville: Broadman Press, 1990).

[5]Isaac McDonald, "Evangelism," *Proclaim,* April-May-June 1989, 31.

[6]Robert Sheffield, *The Ministry of Baptist Deacons* (Nashville: Convention Press, 1990). This book may be purchased at Baptist Book Stores or by calling toll-free 1-800-458-BSSB.

[7]J. Truman Brown and Jere Allen, *Church and Community Diagnosis Workbook* (Nashville: Convention Press, 1986). This book may be purchased at Baptist Book Stores or by calling toll-free 1-800-458-BSSB.

4

Deacons Leading as Change Agents

Robert Sheffield

Robert Sheffield is minister's advocate, LeaderCare Section. LifeWay Church Resources, Nashville, Tennessee.

As we walked along the side of the old auditorium, the deacon stopped and looked at me knowingly. "You know, preacher," he said, "the most dangerous time in the life of a church is a building program." I needed to hear that for several reasons. I inherited a building program for a new auditorium in this first pastorate after seminary. I did not realize the full implications of the changes that would come. I also knew very little about being an effective leader in times of change.

This church faced not only a building program to replace a much-loved auditorium, but also the transition from basically a rural church to a suburban church adjacent to a city of 20,000 people. Thankfully, the building program went well. However, the church only recently began to realize the full potential of the change in the community.

Changes stir up a diverse range of emotions in us. This remains true even though change occurs as the one constant in our lives. We change personally as we go through the various stages of life. Our society changes and probably no more so in the history of the world than now. This statement can be illustrated by the number of items that were not even in existence 50 years ago, such as:[1]

Air Conditioners	Freezers
Antibiotics	Health Insurnace
Automatic Transmissions	Latex Paint
Automatic Washers and Dryers	Magnetic Tape
	Personal Computers
Birth Control Pills	Polio Vaccine
Commercial Jets	Polyester
Compact Discs	Running Shoes
Credit Cards	Safety Belts
Detergents	Smoke Detectors
Disposable Diapers	Supermarkets
Fast Foods	Transparent Tape
Freeze-dried Foods	VCRs

Change involves backward or forward motion. People, things, events, history, or traditions stay the same way for only so long. If progress does not occur, sameness becomes the norm, and retrogression follows.

Change can be difficult. It becomes a challenge for us, therefore, to allow change to happen in a positive way. This is especially true in the life of the church. Most of us say we want our church to grow and prosper. This requires more of us, however, than just our well-wishing. It necessitates the leadership of the church guiding the church through the necessary change for meaningful growth. Since deacons serve as part of the leadership team in the church, deacons need to become leaders capable of both stimulating change and guiding the church through the time of change.

Managing Change

If deacons are to be positive agents for change within the life of the church, they must learn to manage change. Change needs to be managed because it strongly impacts the church. Change tests the fellowship of the church. Since change offers opportunity for disagreement, a church finds out the strength of its fellowship when a proposed change comes up for discussion. This is the reason a building program is a dangerous time in the life of a church. Change can impact the fellowship of our churches negatively unless the process of change receives good guidance.

Change also impacts church growth. Growth in the church requires changes. If your church does not want to make the necessary changes, growth will be hindered. Since most of us can take only so much change at one time, the process of change has to be well managed, permitting the congregation to accommodate the changer.

Congregations have to contend with many types of changes. Some of these include: a community in transition, building of new buildings, remodeling of existing buildings, change of pastors or other staff members, loss of significant volunteer leaders in the church family, significant influx of new members, economic change brought about by the overall economy of the area, age of the membership, different approaches to worship, restructuring of the Sunday School or other church organizations, adding new staff, and the reorientation of the deacons to ministry instead of management. This list, of course, does not cover everything. However, it does cover many of the changes with which our churches have to deal.

Be a Catalyst for Meaningful Change

What place do you, as a deacon, have in managing the change process in the life of the church? You, along with your fellow deacons, can serve in several ways to help manage the change process. For one thing, you serve as a partner with your pastor in being a catalyst for meaningful change. In this role, you and your fellow deacons work with the pastor in getting appropriate change started. This does not mean you dictate to the congregation. At all times you should remember that the biblical model for deacons is servant leadership—not serving as a board of directors. Some of the areas where deacons could serve as catalysts would include church fellowship, stewardship, understanding of Baptist doctrine, care for church members, assimilation of new church members, and certain kinds of organizational issues, such as constitution and bylaws. Again, I want to emphasize that the deacon's role encompasses encouragement and suggestion, not making all the decisions in the areas mentioned.

Share Information Concerning Proposed Changes
Deacons also should be prepared to give information to the congregation concerning proposed changes. An older deacon in a church I pastored often used a phrase which I found unique but very true. Every Friday morning at our prayer breakfast he responded to my greeting by saying, "You can hear everything around here but the truth and meat frying." That was his quaint way of saying that meat was scarce and to be careful about taking at face value what people told me. Details about proposed changes can be altered intentionally and unintentionally as they are passed from one member of the congregation to another. This can cause both confusion and chaos in the change process which, in turn, can lead to fellowship problems. Deacons need to be informed of proposed changes so they can help keep the congregation properly informed and thus keep confusion at a minimum.

Be Willing to Accept Needed Change
Deacons can help the church through change by being personally willing to accept needed change. If your attitude is that of a man I heard at the annual meeting of the Southern Baptist Convention several years ago, you will not be a good leader in change. This man sat in the balcony while a business session of the Convention occurred below. He consistently voted against everything. On one of the votes he shouted toward the speaker's stand, "I am against everything." If this characterizes your attitude, you will not be a good leader for change in your church.

The Nature of Change
To lead through times of change, you can be helped by understanding the types and sources of change. The following remarks relate to change in all situations and not just in a church setting.

Types of Changes
There are several types of change about which we should be aware. Lyle Schaller quotes Thomas R. Bennett in identifying four types of change.

1. *Change in structure.*—This change occurs within the organization in such a way that the essential organization and/or activity undergoes alteration.

2. *Change in technology.*—An illustration of this can be seen in the increased use of computers and television within churches.

3. *Change in behavior.*—Changes in both structure and technology tend to produce changes in behavior.

4. *Change in assumptions and values.*—A change in values and assumptions is essential before either an individual or an organization can be changed substantially.[2]

Leon Martel helps us understand the types of changes by pointing out that some changes are permanent and some cyclical. While the permanent changes require permanent adjustment, the cyclical change, being temporary, requires temporary adjustment.[3] You, as a deacon, need to recognize which is which in the church. Two years ago the section in which I work moved into new offices. These offices provided space for us on a temporary basis. Because it was only temporary, the adjustment to these offices was different than if they had been permanent. This held true for both the pluses and minuses of the new office arrangement.

Sources of Change
It also helps us to consider some of the sources of change. Lyle Schaller indicates three primary sources.

1. *Internally motivated decision.*—The primary motivation for change comes from within the individual or organization. This does not mean, however, that external forces or pressures have not been at work to influence the internally motivated decision.

2. *Externally motivated decision.*—While internal considerations may have a significant impact, the primary motivation for change occurs from without.

3. *Change by indecision.*—A decision on change is postponed

until a change occurs. In these situations it matters little whether the primary forces for change are internal or external.[4]

In examining these sources further, we can see how they operate in the life of a church. Let us use as an example a building program. There will be some in the church who believe strongly in the need for a new building. They speak with conviction in favor of the building because of the need for church growth. These people have probably come to this decision through some external situations in the church. The building won't hold all of the people who come presently and so stymies further growth, or the building is inadequate for worship or teaching the age groups seeking to be reached. Because of internal convictions about church growth, these external situations help them to act out of their primary internal motivation. However, in that same church, some people won't change until they are absolutely forced to or until the whole group votes and they have to go along with it. They don't necessarily own the need internally, but they see the need externally, or it is mandated externally, and they change. Still another group can be seen as those who would put off the change as long as possible until the change has to be made, despite their original objections.

Resistance to Change

Change encounters resistance in most people. Meaningful change cannot happen in your church without some degree of resistance. How do you go about accomplishing the change needed without alienating those who offer the resistance? To do this properly, you must begin by understanding the reasons people become resistant.

Reasons for Resistance

Dr. Bruce Grubbs helps us understand why people resist change.

1. *Threat to security.*—People resist change because of a threat to their sense of security as represented by the predictable and the known. You can understand this quite well when you stop and think that one of the strongest motivators we have is security.

Some people can live with less of it than others, but all people need some. Some people feel they need a stable, nonchanging environment.

2. *Preservation of tradition.*—People resist change out of a reverence for and preservation of that which has grown "holy" through the passage of time. When I served as a pastor, people often resisted changing Sunday School rooms. The class members invested time in decorating the room and soon came to feel possessive about it.

3. *Fear of the unknown.*—People fear losing what is and what can be counted on. Changing the known and trying the unknown becomes more than some people can manage. I have observed this happening in churches who change the order of worship, start a building program, or have an influx of new people into the church family. I was reminded recently, while doing some reading, that we would not have modern day automobiles and airplanes if someone had not been willing to risk something new. The old cliche, "If it isn't broken, don't fix it," may sound good but can lead to a lack of meaningful change.

4. *Loss of control.*—People resist change when it represents a loss of control of their lives and environment. This resistance becomes readily apparent in a church that suddenly starts to grow. A new industry moved into the small town where one such church was located. Even though the people of the church and town said they wanted growth to happen, they tended to shut the newcomers out. Many of the people in the church resisted the change in congregational and fellowship pattern that the new members represented.

5. *Power struggle.*—People resist change because of what can be termed "pride of authorship." This represents a resistance because of competition for power. I have seen some resistance to change occur because the wrong group or person originated the idea, and the pride of other persons or groups could not let the change go unchallenged.

6. *Sense of identity.*—People resist change when it affects their identity. Change may shake a person's sense of who they are and

what role they will occupy in the new group or organization.[5]

Resistance can also have positive benefits. Resistance indicates that people may not have the correct information about the change or understand the ultimate purpose of the change. When resistance occurs, it offers you a good opportunity to clarify your purpose and information flow. The more people understand about the scope and purpose of the change, the better able they are to go along with it. This will be true even if they can't wholeheartedly support the change presented.

Resistance may also indicate a need to develop a better plan. Not all resistance comes from a desire to see the status quo maintained. Sometimes resistance can help plans evolve into something better. I remember a deacon resisting plans presented by the building committee. This deacon not only resisted but offered some suggestions at the business meeting and presented a motion for the matter to be sent back to the committee for further study. The motion carried and the resulting restudy by the committee resulted in a better building project for the church.

Responses to Resistance
Resistance can be a positive force if you, as a leader in change, respond properly. To see how we can respond properly, let's begin by looking at some inappropriate responses to resistance.

1. *Defensiveness.*—Whenever you, as a leader, become defensive toward the person offering the resistance, you will not be able to listen and respond properly. Seek to put the good of the church before getting "my way."

2. *Censoring.*—A person should not be rebuked because they voiced their opinion concerning a proposed change.

3. *Controlling.*—A common way to handle resistance involves controlling the processes in such a way that the resistance loses opportunity to be heard.

4. *Ignoring.*—This approach guarantees trouble for the future. Resistance ignored does not go away.

5. *Punishing.*—This response to resistance leads you to take revenge toward those who have offered the resistance.

6. *Fleeing.*—Some people respond to resistance by becoming a hermit and not responding openly at all. These people would tend to give up the quest for change, retreat from leadership, and let someone else get the change implemented.

If you should not respond in these ways, how should you respond?

Begin by learning how to recognize resistance. We can listen carefully to what people say. A few of the ways people express resistance include:

" 'What we are doing works; why tamper with it?'
'I couldn't change if I wanted to.'
'We can't.'
'That's a good idea, but it won't work for me.'
'Yes, but . . .'
'We just don't do things that way.' "

We also need to look at the body language of the person talking. Arms folded across the chest, eyes closed during the presentation, or eyes wandering during the presentation, all give clues to the mind-set of the person in question. "Silence and withdrawal often signal resistance. On the other extreme, boisterous talk and over-reacting to what is said or done can indicate resistance."[6]

Elaine Dickson helps us by listing the following suggestions:

- "Expect resistance as both natural and desirable.
- Listen to resistance to understand it.
- Take resistance seriously and learn from it."[7]

Reasons for Change

We turn now to the process that enables change to take place in a meaningful and orderly fashion. It would be good for us to reflect a moment on the fact that some change can be unnecessary. Changing only for change's sake does not constitute a valid reason. There can be right and wrong reasons for considering and pursuing a change.

Wrong Reasons for Change
- Satisfying ego needs.

- Imitating others.
- Gaining new leadership.
- Tinkering.[8]

It would be helpful for us to look at each one of these individually. Seeking change to satisfy our own ego is not a good reason. We could want the change because we want to exercise our power, establish our position, or to enhance our reputation. Sometimes projects have started in churches more for those reasons than because they were needed at the time. We also should not try to change just because some other church has done it. This can lead to a competitive spirit between churches. It also does not take into account the fact that every church has a different personality with different needs. Sometimes change occurs because the person leading is new and wants to immediately recreate things. "The inexperienced often try to change too much, too soon."[9] We need to be careful of tinkering with things because we want to or are bored with the way it presently exists. While stability can lead to a rut, it can also lead to a confident working atmosphere. Everyone needs some stability.

Right Reasons for Change

What then constitute some right reasons for change? Bruce Grubbs helps us understand these reasons.

1. *Beliefs are worth initiating change.*—When persons hold incorrect or incomplete views as to the nature of the Christian life or the purpose of the church, change is worth pursuing.

2. *Behavior is worth engaging change.*—When individuals and groups within the church fail or refuse to be guided by the biblical qualities of Christian conduct, a call for change becomes appropriate.

3. *Organizations and procedures that can be improved should be.*—Some structures and ways in which people do their work may limit the church's effectiveness or fail to promote the greatest outcome and are candidates for change.

4. *Goals sometimes mandate change.*—This could be because the wrong goals have been set and need to be changed. It could

also be because recently adopted goals call for change.

5. *Methods require change.*—How a church carries on its work may need to be changed. If a method consistently produces poor results, it probably would be good to explore how it can be changed.[10]

In addition to these reasons, I have added the following categories of positive change opportunities:

6. *Change should enable the inclusion of more people.*—Knowingly or unknowingly, many churches exclude some people from their fellowship. It may be a person with a handicap or one who is different socially, culturally, economically, or ethnically from the majority of the congregation. Sometimes the exclusion occurs simply because the congregation fails to respond properly to new members. The inclusion of more people requires a change in behavior, attitude, and/or buildings.

7. *Change should provide opportunities for service.*—More people, especially new members, should be included in places of service within the church. This could call for changes in methods and organization, as well as attitude.

8. *Change should reflect a growth attitude.*—Growth rather than maintenance should be the characteristic attitude within the church. Paul Powell quotes a deacon in the church he pastored as saying that most institutions and movements eventually go through three stages. "They begin as risktakers, then they grow to be caretakers, and eventually they end up as undertakers."[11] A maintenance attitude can be equated with the caretaker phase. Unless change occurs, the undertaker phase will come. To keep this from happening, a change in attitude and behavior must occur for church growth to happen.

Keys to Effective Change

If deacons are to effectively lead the church in or through change, they should follow these principles.

1. *Recognize that change comes in many different forms.*— "Some changes are like building an addition onto an already completed house—something is added not because it is missing but

because what is there is not adequate.

"Other changes are like rain; they come uninvited, bring enrichment and refreshment, or 'spoil our picnic.'

"Many changes require us to give up what now exists to put something new in its place, like removing old garments from the closet to make space for the new."[12]

2. *The leadership must be properly prepared for leading in the change.*—This leadership includes you, as a deacon, as well as the pastor, staff, and unordained church volunteers. This preparation would include understanding all of the aspects of the change process and how they apply to your specific church situation.

3. *The congregation needs to be led to have a sense of mission purpose.*—Many congregations resist some or all change because of an inadequate sense of biblical mission. A sense of mission will enable the congregation to better see and accept changes in traditions and familiar patterns.

4. *Change occurs best when it is anticipated.*—How that anticipation occurs is important. Leon Martel helps us understand this when he notes the following:

• "Rarely, however, do present trends continue and then only very briefly. While much can be learned from the present, to rely on it to anticipate the future is to miss the changes that are essential to understanding what is to come."

• We should not plan the future by the past. This approach involves making "plans using 'business as usual' as a baseline projection."[13]

Some change will catch the church unaware. A natural disaster comes under this heading. However, many changes can be anticipated and planned for if we follow the proper change procedures.

5. *The process of change needs to be managed so that negative conflict does not occur.*—Change will not occur without some conflict. In fact, conflict should not be avoided because it offers the best way to make the clearest decisions regarding the change. You and others who lead the church in times of change need to learn to be effective conflict managers. If the aim of the church leadership is to avoid all conflict, needed communication will be stifled. The

result of this will be to drive the conflict "underground" and cause long-term damage to the fellowship of the church.

6. *All change costs something.*—This cost may be open, or it may be hidden. Elaine Dickson helps us understand some of the hidden costs concerning change.

"Examples of some of the high costs of change are grief, tension, and stress.

● "Grief— . . . Change means something old has to be given up wholly or partially for something new. . . .

● "Tension— . . . Tension can be illustrated with a rubber band. Put too much tension on it and it pops. Put too little or no tension on it and it simply doesn't do the things a rubber band is meant to do. Put moderate tension on it, and it does the job of holding things together. . . .

● "Stress— . . . Prolonged periods of unremitting stress can create a condition called burnout—exhaustion accompanied by a sense of futility. Each of us has a responsibility to control the cost of change for ourselves and to help control the cost for others."[14]

7. *The appropriate change process needs to be chosen.*—A number of ways exist to bring about change. One way involves announcing the change and assuming people will go along with it. Some deacon groups approach change this way when they make decisions for the congregation.

The most effective way to bring about change embraces a process of congregational participation. The more people involved in all phases of the planned change, the more involvement you will have in implementing the change. Since congregational participation requires more time, planning for a change needs to start early enough to provide for unhurried processes and discussion.

8. *Change within the church works best when we use "sanctified common sense."*—That is another way of saying you should seek the revelation of God's guidance in addition to any reasoning you might bring to bear on the subject of change. In this and other matters in the church we need to claim the promise made to Jeremiah by God: "Call unto me, and I will answer thee, and shew thee great and mighty things, which thou knowest not" (Jer. 33:3). This

keeps us from sitting in our committees and doing little more than pooling our ignorance. It also keeps us in touch with God's purposes for the church. This will help us to keep from doing those things which tend to be the most comfortable according to mere human reasoning.

Steps in Planned Change

What are some steps deacons can follow to enable planned change to occur in your church?

1. *See the need for change.*—The leaders and congregation must see the need for change. This occurs through proper analysis and by sensitizing the congregation to the need for change. It is in this step that effective long-range planning should occur. The Baptist Sunday School Board has a wide array of resources to help a church accomplish planning for the next five years.

2. *Set priorities.*—Since all change is not equally important and cannot all be done at the same time, priorities must be set. This step includes managing the amount of change a congregation undergoes in a specific period of time. Too much change too quickly causes stress for people and organizations. When this kind of stress occurs within the church, negative conflict can often result.

3. *Be committed.*—Those who will be involved with the change must be committed. People support best that in which they feel an ownership. To put it another way, people do not normally get excited in the pursuit of someone else's goals.

4. *Communicate.*—Careful, consistent communication should be planned and carried out all through the change process. This communication needs to take into consideration that some people within the congregation will disagree with the proposed change. The communication, then, needs to be given in a positive, redemptive, and objective manner.

5. *Implement.*—Implementation constitutes the last step. If the other steps have been done properly, this step will be easier. It still should not be assumed that the congregation will wholeheartedly accept the change. Depending on the scope of the change, many people may still resist. Because of this, even the implemen-

tation needs to be done with a redemptive spirit.

Deacons as Change Agents

Certain personal characteristics will make you a good change agent.

Commitment.—I mention this characteristic first because it is a priority. You must possess a strong commitment to the Lord Jesus Christ as Savior and Lord and to the mission of the church. This commitment needs to be strong enough to enable you to put the Lord's will for your life and the church's life first. This commitment leads you to proper faith. Out of this faith comes the ability to guide the church through times of change.

Openness.—You, as a deacon, need to be open to change. You need to feel a sense of wanting change in your personal life that will keep you growing stronger and more effective spiritually and mentally. In order to be open you will have a willingness to allow and encourage change within the church even though you experience some inconvenience. If you are not willing to give up your Sunday School room so the Sunday School can progress, sing new songs that appeal to a wider range of people, and any one of a number of other actions, don't expect others in the church to be different.

Vision.—Deacons need to share a vision for the church with the pastor and staff. What kind of vision do you have for the church in which you serve? When you have a vision, you see more than the present situation. For you, the best is always yet to be. Even though the vision has to be defined, refined, and put into workable form, it precedes successful change. Without a vision you and the church become the captive of habits, traditions, and lazy comfortableness. Where do you get a vision? Through a faith-filled look around. You ask the Holy Spirit to enable you to see through eyes of faith the possibilities for the church.

Boldness.—Any change involves a certain amount of risk. If you cannot or will not risk, you cannot be an effective change agent. This boldness allows you to handle the criticism that comes your way. As an agent of change you need to be willing to support change even though there are those who oppose it, at least in the beginning.

Teammanship.—You and your fellow deacons would do well to remember that you serve as part of a team composed of the pastor, staff, and Church Council.

At no time should any person or group consider their own wants, wishes, ideas, or feelings in isolation from the rest of the team. As a group of deacons you can show the way for the congregation by having an attitude of cooperation and not competition.

Peacemaker.—During the process of change deacons need to be peacemakers. Since change inevitably brings conflict within the church, you and your fellow deacons should try to influence the conflict toward positive results by allowing the Holy Spirit to lead you to exhibit peacemaker characteristics. In this way, the change process has the opportunity to be a positive, growing, God-glorifying experience in the church.

Now that we have looked together at the different facets of deacons leading in times of change, the rest is up to you. For some of you the very act of being an effective change agent requires that you change in some significant ways. While you may find this difficult, the results will be rewarding. You will not only grow personally, but you will also enable the church to reach its ultimate potential.

Throughout my more than 30 years of pastoral ministry, I have experienced deacons along the whole spectrum of change responsiveness. My memory holds two deacons in particular. One served in a church I pastored. The other attended a conference I led a number of years ago. The first deacon was in his early 70s. He and his wife had no children. His vision encompassed the need our church had for new pre-school facilities. He did not need them personally but inspired and encouraged the church to build them. The other deacon stood at the end of a conference on church growth and said, "To tell you the truth, I don't want our church to grow." He went on to explain that he did not want to go through what it would take for the church to grow. After which one of these deacons will you pattern your leadership style? I encourage you to let it be the first and to recommit yourself to allowing the Lord to help you accomplish it.

[1]William J. Pfeiffer, Leonard D. Goodstein, and Timothy M. Nolan, *Shaping Strategic Planning* (San Diego: University Associates, 1989), 3.

[2]Lyle M. Schaller, *The Change Agent* (Nashville: Abingdon Press, 1972), 35-38.

[3]Leon Martel, *Mastering Change* (New York: New American Library, 1986), 28.

[4]Schaller, 39-41.

[5]Joe R. Stacker and Bruce Grubbs, *Pastoral Leadership for Growing Churches* (Nashville: Convention Press, 1988), 55-57.

[6]Elaine Dickson, *Say No, Say Yes to Change* (Nashville: Broadman Press, 1982), 87.

[7]Ibid., 87-93.

[8]James J. Cribbin, *Leadership* (New York: AMACON, 1981), 191-92.

[9]Ibid., 192.

[10]Stacker and Grubbs, 58-59.

[11]Paul W. Powell, *Go-Givers in a Go Getter World* (Nashville: Broadman Press, 1986), 11.

[12]Dickson, 59-60.

[13]Martel, 255-57.

[14]Dickson, 126-29.

5
Deacons Leading in Times of Transition

Charles Belt

Charles Belt is a businessman living in Charlottesville, Virginia.

To live is to change. To change is to experience transition. Just as individuals experience transition, churches also confront the challenge to step into the unknown, to move beyond the existing parameters of doing life, and to answer the invitation to participate in new and different experiences. What is the church to do in the face of the challenge of transition? What role do deacons play in leading the church in times of transition? What are those transitions that congregations encounter, and how can a congregation be led to respond to the call to participate?

Transition is defined in Webster's Dictionary as a "passage from one state, stage, subject or place to another."[1] Obviously, we experience some passages because of our own choices and the resulting consequences of those choices. At other times, we experience transition because we are forced by the decisions and actions of other persons to participate in moving into the unfamiliar. And still other times, life itself seems to move us beyond where we are. Fault lies with no person or experience or decision. Life simply progresses, and we are caught up in its movement.

From time to time we're going to confront major transitional periods. No relationship remains the same forever. People grow up. People change. People die. Places, opportunities, and events are all subject to modification and change.

Because deacons are a vital part of the pastoral ministries leadership team within the church, they play a major role in the process of enabling a congregation to understand and negotiate its way through the various transitions encountered and to accomplish its mission in the world.

What are some of the transition experiences churches encounter, and how can deacons minister in these times of transition? Two examples follow.

Transition: A Change of Pastors

In January of 1986, the Research Services Department of the Baptist Sunday School Board released the results of a study entitled *Negotiating Expectations in Ministry*.[2] The introductory paragraph referred to the Webster's Dictionary definition of *negotiation* in terms of bringing about an agreement through conference, discussion, and compromise. In the context of this definition, the study revealed that "very little negotiating (in the sense of give and take) is actually going on in the process of ministers changing churches." Two reasons were cited. First, ministers desiring to move basically rely on "the good-faith principle" of God's people. The good-faith principle expresses the idea that if both the minister and the church sense God's leadership in a possible union, questions and involved discussions seem unimportant. Ministers simply assume the church will deal fairly with them. Second, ministers desiring to move are not going to deliberately bring up unwelcome or sensitive issues which might turn off the interview process and hinder the chances of moving to that church. Ministers want to look good for the committee.

My experience has been that this is a two-way street. Search committees interested in a particular candidate do not want to expose any of the church's blemishes for fear that such exposure will make them appear undesirable.

So, both the candidate and the committee are in what Loren

Mead describes as a "double bind." Both are putting their best foot forward trying to positively impress one another while at the same time trying to get an accurate picture of one another in order to make a sound decision.[3] What actually happens, as the research reveals, is avoidance of the issues at the heart of positive church-pastor relationships that build health and long tenure resulting in positive church growth. Issues and concerns that both the pastor and the committee are concerned about do not get discussed before a decision is made to call the pastor/accept the church's call. I believe much of the conflict resulting in short tenure could be avoided altogether if pastors and search committees would get real with each other from the very start.

A growing desire between ministers and churches is to stay together longer. Pastoral tenure is increasing. In 1985, the pastoral tenure across the Southern Baptist Convention was 2.8 years. Today, it is about 4.6 years. As encouraging as that increase is, there also continues to be an alarming increase in the numbers of forced terminations. This suggests to me that in addition to choosing termination as a way of resolving conflict, churches and ministers are not discussing many of the issues during the pre-call negotiation period which are becoming centers of conflict later on.

I believe deacons can administer strategic service during this critical period before a church extends a call to a prospective pastor. The time without a pastor is generally viewed by the church as a necessary evil and time that should be as brief as possible. I visited a church in search of a pastor. Without a pastor for about 10 weeks, the church had just voted to call an interim pastor. As I talked with one of the deacons, he was almost apologetic over the fact that it had taken so long to get an interim pastor. He assured me that at the same time, the search committee was really working hard to, as he said, "hurry up and get a good preacher, because no church can do much without a preacher." I cringed at the statement because it reflects what far too many churches believe—that the time without a pastor is a time when everything gets put on hold until a new pastor is on the field. As we talked, I reflected on the great opportunity the church has during a pastorless period to really take a fresh look at itself and come to terms with what kind of future it desires to experience.

Taking such a forward look involves understanding the dynamics at work when a pastor leaves and then coming to terms with a number of critical engagements churches must face before extending a call to a new pastor.

Dynamics Involved When a Pastor Leaves

Whenever a pastor leaves, his departure triggers a wide range of emotions both congregationally and individually.

Congregational Emotions

One lady, upon hearing the news that her pastor was leaving, declared: "I can't believe it. What are we going to do without a pastor!" This belief that the pastor would not leave and fear over an uncertain future are often experienced by the congregation when a pastor leaves. Often, it is feared that the programs of a church will cease or fall apart without pastoral leadership. Anxiety over administrative matters and questions about leadership within the church also surface when a pastor leaves. Congregations can feel betrayed and become angry over a pastor's decision to leave. A profound sense of loss is felt by most congregations when their pastor leaves even if the circumstances around his departure are sensitive and difficult. A sense of momentary panic can also grip a congregation as it realizes that it must now begin to take actions and make decisions that have previously been carried out by the pastor. Questions like, "What are we going to do?" or "How are we going to get all the things done that need to be done?" or "Who is going to be in charge now?" or "What's this going to do to our ministry in the community?" are all questions that express a wide range of emotions that congregations experience when the pastor leaves.

Individual Emotions

There is a personal side to this dynamic. A pastor's departure triggers a wide range of emotions and responses from individuals within a congregation. Some members will simply say good-bye and express their appreciation; while others will move into places of responsibility for providing leadership in worship and other pastoral services. Some church members will be delighted at the pastor's departure; while others will mourn his leaving. Everyone will wonder about the future, and some will begin to intentionally plan for that future. Others will simply withdraw from active participation and wait to see in which direction the church moves. Previously inactive members might seize the opportunity to move into key positions of leadership. Anger and guilt over the pastor's leaving will characterize some members; while others express a sigh of relief. A pastor's departure surfaces all kinds of feelings and responses, both positive and negative.

Deacons will also experience some of these feelings. As they come to understand the dynamics of their particular transition experience in the life of the church, however, they will be in a position for vital ministry and leadership to the church. Deacons can help the church to remain strong and healthy during the period between pastors.

What Can Deacons Do?

At some point, the process for searching for a new pastor will begin. A number of very fine resources are available to help churches establish and train a pastor search committee to lead the church in calling a pastor. Here are a few of these resources for your assistance:

- *The Pastor Selection Committee*. Nashville: Sunday School Board, 1977.
- *Pastor Search Committee*. Gerald M. Williamson. Nashville: Broadman Press, 1981.
- *When a Pastor Search Committee Comes, Or Doesn't*. J. William Harbin. Nashville: Broadman Press, 1985.
- *Your Work on the Pulpit Committee*. Leonard Hill. Nashville: Broadman Press, 1970.
- *When a Pastor Leaves*. J. William Harbin. Brentwood: Tennessee Baptist Convention, 1980.

- *Seeking and Calling a Pastor.* Clifton Perkins. Jackson, Mississippi: Mississippi Baptist Convention.

This is by no means an exhaustive list of resources to help the pastor search committee. Many state conventions offer helps that have been developed within their convention offices. Directors of missions also may provide valuable help. Whichever process is decided upon, any church can move through a sequence of steps leading to the calling of a pastor. However, because of the sensitive nature of the interim period in the life of a church, and in light of the great potential it holds for a church's future health and growth, great care should be taken at the very beginning to guide the church through this period of transition.

Deacons can minister valuable service in three areas.

Support the Search Committee

Deacons can work closely with the search committee to guide the church through certain issues and questions that emerge when a church is without a pastor. Loren Mead describes several developmental tasks that every church should give attention to before calling a new pastor.[4]

- Help the church to come to terms with its history and discover a new identity. Every church has a history and an identity. However, the need to understand the deeper story of a church becomes critical as a church stands on the threshold of its future. A church out of touch with its history and identity will not be able to accurately determine where it wants to go or what kind of pastor it will take to lead it into that future.

Deacons might lead in a series of meetings at the church to talk about what the congregation is like and why, where it wants to go, and what kind of leader is needed to realize those dreams. Members can be encouraged to talk about what their church has meant to them in the past and why.

These kinds of encounters can do much to help congregations come to terms with their own history and how they see themselves at this critical point in the life of the church. Such encounters can prompt the realization that perhaps a different kind of leader is needed now to take the church into the next chapter of its life and ministry.

• Allow needed leadership change. When a pastor leaves a church, there is a shift in the leadership of the church. Generally, those who favor a particular pastor will move into key leadership positions during his tenure. Those who, for different reasons, do not favor the pastor's leadership, tend to step into the shadows for as long as that pastor leads the church. These folks may become a resistant force opposing the pastor or just become silent members, present but uninvolved. Some folks may have been overlooked for leadership positions and, when a pastor leaves, step to the forefront again to try to win a leadership position. At the same time, those who have been active under the pastor may take advantage of an opportunity to step down and take a much-needed rest. And, of course, there are always needs for new leadership to be discovered within the congregation, and the pastor's departure will mark the beginning of this search as well.

Deacons play a major role in the process of leadership changes in the church. They are themselves involved in some of the changes. Therefore, deacons can help encourage the needed changes and give direction to the congregation as members deal with new opportunities for service as well as struggle with the decision to remain in positions of leadership or step aside and allow others to become more involved.

• Look to the denomination for help. Mead says that the time between pastors can also be a time of clarifying and redefining the church's connection with its denomination and association. Some churches are not aware of the help that the denomination offers churches when they move through the experience of being without a pastor. Many state convention offices assist churches in securing interim pastors, establishing and training pastor search committees, and providing help in locating prospective candidates.

Deacons can take a vital leadership role in helping the church build a strong relationship with denominational offices as well as associational leadership. Directors of missions are a vital resource to a church during a pastorless period, and deacons can open the door for assistance from their DOM. Generally, directors of missions are knowledgeable of the church's history and identity and can provide sensitive guidance for the church during this time. Directors of missions are vital links between the local church and denominational resources. I have always appreciated and benefited from directors of missions' ministry at this point.

Deacons should stress the value and importance of a denomination as they help the search committee do its work. Most churches discover a new sense of pride and appreciation of their denomination as they access this primary resource when a pastor leaves.

• Encourage commitment to new directions and ministry. Whenever a church sets out to find a pastor, one thing is guaranteed up front: Given time and persistence, it will find, call, and move a new pastor into the church field. However, what is not guaranteed from the outset is whether or not any of those things will make a difference in the quality of life, relationship, and ministry of the church.

The real purpose for engaging these tasks is to ensure that, in fact, it will make a difference in terms of pastoral tenure, congregational health, and balanced biblical growth enabling the church to accomplish its mission. It means that in the final analysis, a church will have learned a lot about itself, its history, and its potential and will have determined who it is and where it wants to go. In addition, it means that the search committee and congregation will be better equipped to make difficult decisions regarding the kind of pastoral leadership the church needs and more willing to talk about the gutsy issues related to the relationship between the pastor and the church. Ultimately, it means that when a pastor stands in the pulpit to preach his first sermon as pastor of the church, it represents more than just his first Sunday. Rather, it marks the beginning of a whole new chapter for the church and the community.

This particular meantime period in the life of the church demands and deserves all of the creative energy a congregation can harness and certainly provides one of the greatest challenges deacons will face in their servant leadership of the church.

Care for the Congregation

Deacons can also maintain pastoral care of the congregation. Paul wrote in 2 Corinthians 1:3-4: "What a wonderful God we have—he is the Father of our Lord Jesus Christ, the source of every mercy, and the one who so wonderfully comforts and strengthens us in our hardships and trials. And why does he do this? So that when others are troubled, needing our sympathy and encouragement, we can pass on to them this same help and comfort God has given us" (TLB).[5]

When a pastor leaves, there are certainly members who are troubled and in need of sympathy and encouragement. I have already mentioned the grief and profound sense of loss that some church members experience when their pastors leave. These needs continue on into the interim period when a church is without a pastor. In addition, there continue to be other pastoral care needs in the lives of the church family. As servant leaders, deacons can attend to many of these pastoral needs of the people which would ordinarily be attended to by a pastor. This does not mean that deacons are to become pastors. The term *pastor* designates a position within the church. *Pastoral* refers to the shepherding of the flock of God. In this latter sense, every Christian can engage in pastoral activities. Deacons especially can offer a redemptive, loving leadership to the church family when a pastor is not available. Not only will such a ministry help the individuals in specific need, but it will also serve to strengthen the fellowship of the church.

"The aim of biblical ministry is to help accomplish Christ's mission on earth."[6] Toward this end, deacons are key leaders in the church. When there is no pastor to lead in caregiving activities, deacons must assume the responsibility and see to it that the work gets done.

Maintain Good Worship Services

Deacons should also work to maintain worship experiences that hold forth hope for a bright future in Christ Jesus. The pastor had been gone from the church for about six weeks when one of the deacons commented to the director of missions, "Oh boy, we surely do need to hurry up and get a pastor. Our worship services are awful. We can't even have a decent service without a preacher!"

When a church is without a pastor, there is a fear that the program of ministry within the church, including the worship experiences on Sundays, will come to a grinding halt or that the quality will become so poor that folks won't want to come.

When a pastor leaves and the church begins to wrestle with the fears that the church will not be able to hold on without a pastor, deacons must lead out in walking toward that fear declaring two things. (1) The deacons also struggle with this nagging fear, but it's OK. Fear is a normal emotion in our lives. The fear is not what causes our difficulty but rather how we perceive our fear and whether or not we let that fear control us in our decisions and actions. (2) Deacons can and must declare the hope for our sustaining power in Christ and lead out in communicating this message through the worship experiences from week to week during the interim period without a pastor.

Deacons can do several things to lead out in worship services. (1) Become involved in planning worship services. (2) Become visible as active participants in the worship experiences. (3) Be willing to preach, if necessary. I know more deacons who have the ability to proclaim the gospel from the pulpit if they would just be willing than I know deacons who want to preach but lack the ability to do it. (4) Greet worshipers (members and visitors alike) with a warm and expectant spirit. (5) Be sensitive to the environment of the worship setting. (6) Be alert during the service to notice the movement of God's Spirit. Opportunities for counseling should always be detected and followed up during the invitation or even after the worship service is over. (7) Share from the pulpit weekly words of encouragement to the congregation.

The period between pastors is always a delicate time for a church family. Churches need to use the time to get in touch with who and what they really are and what they believe and desire the nature of their future to be under God's leadership and under the leadership of a new pastor.

The time between pastors can be a time of shoring up personal relationships within the church. Care needs to be given to the fellowship and personal needs of individuals. Worship services need to be positive, hopeful experiences encouraging the church family in their faith.

Deacons can be leaders in all of these dimensions of church life during this time. In addition, they can lead the church to affirm the church's staff. A pastor's departure should never automatically signal a movement to "get rid of" other staff also. Far too often, we undermine God's call of church staff by allowing the new pastor the freedom to automatically "clean house," as it were. Such agreements are often made during the search committee's interview with a prospective pastor. Great care should be taken to prevent the automatic removal of church staff when a new pastor comes to the field.

Transition: Changing Community

A community in transition is a community where the basic character of the community is changing. Basic to the character of any community is its racial, ethnic, socioeconomic, and life-style makeup. When these elements begin to change dramatically from what has been considered to be a norm over the years, that community can be identified as being in transition.

Characteristics of a Changing Community

Churches located in changing communities generally exhibit several characteristics, including the following:

- A business-as-usual agenda resulting in stagnation and decline.
- A faded dream resulting in the loss of the sense of mission.
- A nostalgic remembrance of the "good old days."
- A large percentage of members over the age of 55 years.[7]

Many Southern Baptist churches located in metropolitan areas are experiencing transitional symptoms. For example, some churches are experiencing dramatic life-style transitions, the most difficult of the various types of transitions to define.

Life-style transitions might mean a migration of urban life-style groups into previously rural areas or the slow evolutionary transition that occurs almost unnoticeably in a community, such as when households once filled with young children and families become households of "empty nesters." "The church in the changing community is that church whose facility is located in a community where the basic, traditional characteristics have experienced or are experiencing dramatic transition."[8]

What can deacons do when members begin to declare: "This is not the church I grew up in. What happened to my church?"

Stages in the Life Cycle of the Community

Understanding a community in transition is helped when we understand the stages through which most communities develop and the life cycle or stages in the life of a church.

1. *Newly developing stage.*—Patterns of relating economically, socially, culturally, and religiously become established in a new residential neighborhood. Early on, it's easier to draw people into the church than when the community stabilizes as years pass.

2. *Periods of stability.*—The makeup of a community is set and relatively homogeneous.

3. *Pre-transitional stage.*—The makeup of a community begins to shift. New groups begin moving in. Present racial, ethnic, or life-style groups begin moving out. While the new groups comprise a relatively small percentage of the total community population, their numbers will increase. Some of the churches will attempt to reach out to these new groups. Most churches will not.

4. *Transitional stage.*—New groups in the community are now as much as 50 percent of the population. Change is more rapid, creating greater resistance and conflict from those who represent what the community used to be. Neighborhood churches experience greater numbers of their membership moving out of the community, yet they resist establishing new strategies to reach out to the new groups.

5. *Post-transitional stage.*—The community is old, but residents are new.[9] Davis and White indicate that the stage can actually represent the vital, newly developing stage for the new groups in the old community.[10] Therefore, the cycle begins to repeat itself.

However, the churches of the community may still be made up of the power structure of the old community and church population—very resistant to all the transition. Some of these churches will relocate, merge, disband—and some will try to reach the new community. Some will succeed while others will simply continue to decline and die.

Stages in the Life Cycle of the Church[11]
Just as a community goes through various stages, so does a church. A brief review of these stages follows.

1. *Birth.*—The birth of a new church theoretically corresponds to the newly developing stage of a community. The dream for a new work becomes a reality as people gather to form a new church.

2. *Development.*—During this period, the church forms its norms and beliefs and formulates its unique mission in the community. It sets goals and develops an organizational structure to enable it to effectively meet those goals. As the community stabilizes, so does the church and its programs of ministry in the community.

3. *Maturity.*—This is the period when the ministry is being conducted in such a way that the church is realizing its mission and living out its dream. Membership may reach its high point during this time. The community continues its period of stability or may begin to move into pretransitional stages. However, for a while at least, the church will not sense or feel the subtle changes beginning to occur in the community.

4. *Decline.*—Why a church moves into a period of decline is a more complex issue than the pretransitional dynamics of a community. A church may decline as a result of community changes, as a result of its original dream being fulfilled, as a result of inter-

nal conflict that splits the membership, as a result of its own re-sisting the normal process of changing, or as a result of failing to plan for its future or to sustain growth. Eventually, the signs of decline become visible and the congregation takes notice of the changing realities. Theoretically, this period follows similarly the transitional stage in community development. Congregational concern heightens, and questions as to why all this is happening are asked. Financial realities are brought to bear on the programs and operations of the church and even on the ability of the church to maintain its ministerial staff.

5. *Death or redevelopment.*—As with the post-transitional changes in community development, this stage in the life cycle of a church can mean the difference in whether that church redis-covers its mission and ministry or continues to decline and ulti-mately die.

What Can Deacons Do?

Churches choose to decline or die. Any church can choose to sur-vive, change, and redeem its dream. Any church can establish and/or reestablish ministry to the community around it and be-gin to effectively serve the people within reach of its ministry arm. How can deacons help?

1. Deacons can help a church move through the periods of tran-sition that mark the passage from one stage of its life cycle to the next.

2. Deacons can help the church understand the dynamics of community changes and how those changes impact the life of the church.

3. Deacons can be sensitive to emotional factors involved in a congregation facing a changing community. A congregation fac-ing a changing community can encounter many of the same emo-tions experienced by individuals who are dying or are dealing with the death of someone close in their family or a beloved friend: denial, independence, isolation, anger, resentment, bargaining, and depression.

4. Deacons can work with the pastor and staff to lead the

church into an intensive self-study project to help the church to get in touch with its changing environment and to begin to take steps to ensure the church's survival and effective ministry efforts. Resources to help the church experience meaningful transition would include: (1) *Kingdom Principles Growth Strategies* module and (2) *To Dream Again.*[12]

5. Deacons can help lead the church to determine the direction it wants to take in dealing with the changing community. Several alternatives are possible at this point.[13]

• To remain in the community without changing and survive as long as it can.

• To remain in the community, changing to meet the changing community character and makeup.

• To merge with a nearby church, joining forces to effectively minister to the changing community.

• To relocate. Relocation is complex and should be given long, intensive, and prayerful consideration. Ezra Earl Jones says a church may justifiably relocate as long as: (1) those people remaining in the community have access to a church similar in denomination; (2) the church will not be moving away from more of its members than it is moving toward; (3) the decision is overwhelmingly a congregational majority decision; (4) the area it is moving to has real need for a church of its denomination anyway; and (5) there is an adequate and affordable site on which to relocate.[14] In addition, the director of missions in the association out of and/or into which the church is moving should be consulted. In other words, what will it mean to all concerned if the church is no longer here but somewhere else.

• To disband.

We have examined only two of the transitional experiences churches encounter. In each case, deacons play a major role in helping to guide the church through the transitional period and to remain a strong witness for Christ.

There is no easy passage through the maze of transition and change. Nonetheless, reality demands that we encounter each transition occurrence with faith in the One who holds our future secure. Deacons are leaders in the church, spiritual leaders called and gifted "for such a time as this" (Esth. 4:14).

Transition experiences do not spell success or failure of leadership or congregation. To live is to grow. To grow is to change. To change is to move through transition. In each case, whether we become stronger and realize more of that for which we have been "laid hold of by Christ Jesus" (Phil. 3:12, NASB)[15] depends on our choices and actions. Deacons can help the church make the best choices and take the best actions that can lead the church into the next chapter in God's unfolding will for the church. That should be the outcome of every church transition experience.

[1]*Webster's Ninth New Collegiate Dictionary,* s.v. "transition."

[2]Kenneth E. Hayes, *Negotiating Expectations in Ministry,* Research Services Department, Baptist Sunday School Board, 1986.

[3]Loren Mead, *Critical Moment of Ministry: A Change of Pastors* (New York: The Alban Institute, 1986), 28.

[4]Ibid., 37-50.

[5]Verses marked TLB are taken from *The Living Bible.* Copyright ©Tyndale House Publishers, Wheaton, Illinois, 1971. Used by permission.

[6]Robert Sheffield, *The Ministry of Baptist Deacons* (Nashville: Convention Press, 1990), 15.

[7]Jere Allen, *P.A.C.T.,* Metropolitan Missions Department, (Atlanta:) 9.

[8]Ibid., 9

[9]Ibid., 13f.

[10]James H. Davis and Woodie W. White, *Racial Transition in the Church* (Nashville: Abingdon Press, 1980), 54-57.

[11]Bob Dale, *To Dream Again: How to Help Your Church Come Alive* (Nashville: Broadman & Holman Publishers, 1981) discusses in great detail the life cycles through which organizations, including churches, move. Very similar to Dale's analysis, *P.A.C.T.* describes the life cycle of a church in five distinct stages.

[12]Gene Mims and Mike Miller, *Kingdom Principles Growth Strategies* (Nashville: Convention Press, 1995) and Bob Dale, *To Dream Again* (Nashville: Broadman & Holman Publishers, 1986); J. Truman Brown, *Long Range Planning Notebook* (Nashville: Convention Press, 1984).

[13]Allen, 21-26.

[14]Ezra Earl Jones, *Strategies for New Churches* (New York: Harper & Row, 1976), 160-61.

[15]From the *New American Standard Bible.* ©The Lockman Foundation, 1960, 1962, 1963, 1968, 1971, 1972, 1973, 1975, 1977. Used by permission.

6
Deacons Leading with Pastor and Staff

Jerry Songer

Jerry Songer is retired pastor, First Baptist Church, Roswell, Georgia.

The purpose of this chapter is to consider the relationship among the deacons, the pastor, and the staff. The intention of this section is to discuss how we may work practically together to lead the church.

A Biblical Model

The Bible speaks about the pastor and deacons and lay leadership role. I believe Acts 6 is a model for us. Verse 1 says, "In those days when the number of the disciples was increasing, the Grecian Jews among them complained against those of the Aramnic-speaking community because their widows were being overlooked in the daily distribution of food" (NIV).

Here the Bible describes for us the need for leadership. Then, as today, the church often was sidetracked. Everything was not being done. Some of the widows were being neglected. There was inequity. Some were well cared for; others were overlooked.

This is typical. For 30 years I have been a "church watcher." In churches of all kinds, I have observed disagreements. But God's intention is that disagreements be minimum, not maximum.

Sometimes the church is in conflict and confusion by intention. Usually, however, it is unintentional. Regardless, there is a way out of the wilderness. "Read the directions." That's good advise when you don't know what to do. Lets read on in Acts 6.

In verse 2 we read, "So the Twelve gathered all the disciples together and said, 'It would not be right for us to neglect the ministry of the word of God in order to wait on tables' " (NIV). So, the apostles called the multitude together. They assumed their place of leadership. Leadership always involves delegation. The early church put that into practice.

The passage continues: "Brothers, choose seven men from among you who are known to be full of the Spirit and wisdom. We will turn this responsibility over to them and will give our attention to prayer and the ministry of the word" (Acts 6:3-4, NIV).

We are to proclaim the Word. We are also to serve the people. Both are vital. The church must maintain a happy medium. Both extremes must be included. That is not easy. The temptation is for us to emphasize one and to neglect the other. How can we accomplish a balance? Scripture teaches us that we must enlist others to help. We must learn to share our ministry. We must give it away; we must find others who can help. In the front of an old Bible is a motto I wrote a long time ago. "I will not do anything myself that someone else can do as well, or better." The pastor and the staff must share the ministry of the church. The pastor has no choice. If we are going to be faithful to the Word of God, we must give away the ministry that has been given to us.

The word for *choose* in Acts 6:3 is an action word. It describes the guard at his post. He knows safety and success are in his hands. He observes like a hawk. His eyes constantly scan the horizon. He is always alert. He is always on the lookout.

Like a soldier or an air traffic controller in the tower, we must always be on ready alert. Our eyes must be trained to find those whom God has gifted to share in ministry.

In Ephesians 4:11, the apostle Paul says, "It was he who gave some to be apostles, some to be prophets, some to be evangelists, and some to be pastors and teachers, to prepare God's people for works of service, so that the body of Christ may be built up" (NIV). Here is the job description for leaders: prepare God's people for work.

How may we fulfill our calling? God gives the church apostles, prophets, evangelists, pastors and teachers, and deacons as the equippers. These are the player-coaches Elton Trueblood speaks of. We exist for the purpose of helping the church members fulfill their purpose in life. We are not here to be ministered unto. Jesus said we are all here to minister.

God's plan is for pastors and deacons to share together. One complements the other. It is God's way.

In 1 Timothy 3, Paul discussed with Timothy the qualifications for those who lead the church. He described the bishops and deacons. Both have an important place in the church.

First Timothy 3:8 says, "Deacons, likewise, are to be men worthy of respect, sincere, not indulging in much wine, and not pursuing dishonest gain" (NIV). The word *likewise* is a large word. It places a responsibility for the welfare of the church upon the overseer and the deacon.

First Timothy 3:15 says, "if I am delayed, you will know how people ought to conduct themselves in God's household, which is the church of the living God, the pillar and foundation of the truth" (NIV). Here we see Paul's purpose for ministry. He wanted them to know how to behave! That is the bottom line for all we do.

In some churches today the ministers act as if they are the lord of the church. We need to remember that position has already been filled; we are all under the lordship of Jesus Christ. If there is a CEO in the church today, it is not the pastor.

God has called ministers and deacons to be partners together in ministry. That job can best be done when each one gives himself to the task. We are together, yolked with Christ to fulfill His mission on the earth.

In 1 Corinthians 12 Paul speaks about the church's problems. Every church has problems. No church is perfect. It's what you do with what you have that pays off in the end. God has equipped His church with gifts needed for every situation. God has a way to lead

His church out of the wilderness and into the promised land.

First Corinthians 12:28 says, "And in the church God has appointed first of all apostles, second prophets, third teachers, then workers of miracles, also those having gifts of healing, those able to help others, those with gifts of administration, and those speaking in different kinds of tongues" (NIV). Paul here gives us the various positions in the church. They have been set in place by God.

Our granddaughter, Stacey, likes to play checkers. When we put the checkers in their place on the board, we can play the game. In like fashion God has set His people in place in the church. They are no longer out of circulation or on the shelf. Each one in the church has been given his assignment from our Commander-in-Chief. We each have our orders. We have our own directions.

When each of us performs our own function, the church will be meshed together. As a basket is made of many strands, so is the body of Christ. God gave the early church apostles, prophets, teachers, miracle workers, gifts of healing, helps, governments, and diversities of tongues. No one has all of these gifts. So it is only as we assume our rightful place that can God be glorified.

Partners in Conflict Resolution

Perhaps this is the greatest challenge in ministry. When everyone agrees, ministry is a simple matter. The test of a pilot is not how well he can fly a plane on a sunny day. The test of his ability is how well he can fly a plane in stormy weather. The same is true in the church.

How can the church handle the storms of conflict? Some churches try to avoid them altogether. When storm clouds arise, they do nothing. But a pilot can hardly afford that luxury. Sometimes there is no other way than to fly through the storm. Churches, rather than doing nothing, must face their times of turbulence as well.

When I served at Central Baptist Church, Waycross, Georgia, God gave me a special opportunity for dealing with controversy.

The deacons and the church had voted to create a pastorium committee. The existing pastorium was dated and inadequate. The committee recommended a new pastorium be built. The deacons voted 16 to 14 against the motion and recommended to the church that the committee be dissolved.

When the church received the motion, they voted that the church also vote on the same information the deacons had received. Subsequently, the church voted on a Sunday morning by ballot.

At that time, the motion passed to build a new pastorium by a three to two margin, in spite of the deacons' objection. I shall long remember church clerk Ronald Thomas' counsel to me. He said, "You have to decide how many people you want to be upset with you. If the motion is rescinded, two-thirds will be upset. If the motion stands, a third will be. Regardless, some are going to disagree."

But God handled the matter in a marvelous way. The pastorium was built, and within six months of selling the old, the new one was paid for.

What did the pastor and deacons learn in that situation? Both were reminded anew that the church has the final say. When given the proper opportunity, the church can speak clearly about what is right.

Partners in Planning

When I was pastor at Central Baptist Church in Chattanooga, Tennessee, I learned a new way to plan deacon meetings. Doug Jacobs was my teacher. He suggested that the deacon officers and pastor meet on the Wednesday before each deacons meeting. We could then plan together the agenda.

Like a chef preparing a feast, we each brought to that agenda the various aspects of ministry we felt important. While I was able to contribute what I felt was important, I also could see through the eyes of the others. I could hear their perceptions of where we were and where we needed to be.

The deacons meetings, as a result, took on a different tone.

Things didn't just happen. Planning and preparing created a considerable amount of anticipation.

I could hardly wait for our planning meetings. They became creative sessions of sharing together with God's leaders under the leadership of the Holy Spirit. Often regular deacons meetings do not allow enough time for planning. The press of time and schedules preclude creative thinking.

Our church in Roswell has begun a quarterly planning session for deacons on Saturday mornings. Last month we met at 8:30 a.m. for a continental breakfast, and at 9:00 a.m. we had a special planning session. Such special planning sessions can be good for church leaders.

First Baptist Church, Americus, Georgia recently decided on a weekend planning session. My wife and I had the privilege of being their leaders. We were able to have separate sessions on Friday evening and Saturday morning. My wife, Jane, led the ladies while I met with the men.

We were able to deal personally with matters that were especially important to both groups. Affirmations and recognitions were allowed with the luxury of time.

State conventions now offer events that afford a meaningful interchange among deacons, pastors, and staff members. My wife and I have had opportunities of sharing in a number of occasions like this. Usually they are held in tranquil settings, such as Lake Yale and Blue Springs in Florida, which offer excellent motel-like facilities.

The opportunity for interchange among leaders from different churches is most stimulating. I especially enjoyed being at Eagle Eyre in Virginia last year. It has been my privilege to be in Nashville for their state deacons conference. My wife and I have participated at the Norman Park Assembly in South Georgia; D. F. Norman and Bill Harrison had planned an excellent program. Meetings such as these can recharge weak batteries.

Partners in Administration

Considerable amount of ambiguity exists when we discuss ministry and administration in church life. Balance is so important. The pendulum is swinging, I believe.

Early in our church history deacons were especially involved in administration. In most instances, this was done to the neglect of ministry. A hundred years ago, and even 50 years ago, deacons were much more concerned about fiscal and physical matters pertaining to the church. The spiritual matters of ministry were left for the pastor and other staff members.

During the past 25 to 50 years, however, this has changed. Gaines S. Dobbins was a pioneer in this area. Robert Naylor and Howard Foshee, Charles Treadway and Ernest Moseley were other able voices. Their leadership has given rise to a new philosophy of ministry among deacons. We are all ministers-servants. The board of deacons and business manager concept is no longer a viable model.

Now in some places we have gone too far. Some excellent leaders in the church feel uncomfortable. They sense that their business expertise is not wanted in deacon ministry. They feel incapable of meaningful spiritual ministry. This causes some drop-out. Thus their spirit is lost.

Today we see the need for both. Perhaps a new breed of deacon is developing. We need both gifts—ministry and administration—in leadership. Just five years ago I first heard Bruce Grubbs say this. It was such an answer for me. "This ought you to have done and not left the other undone," Jesus says. In our church we are trying to have the best of both worlds.

Our trustees care for all legal matters. These five men have all served as active deacons at one time or another. They keep the deacons and church informed of matters of mutual concern. At the present time they and the finance committee have engaged in a lawsuit over a disputed land contract.

We have a large committee structure in our church. We try to have at least one deacon on each committee, but it is not a requirement. We seek to have the best persons serving in the capacities that are needed. Each committee is responsible for fulfilling the job description as approved by the church.

In matters of major concerns that may affect the spiritual life of the church, deacons are involved. Their counsel is often sought. They may or may not vote to endorse a committee's report before it is brought to the church for authorization and implementation.

Deacons meetings are primarily for the purposes of carrying on matters of ministry and concerns among the total church. Deacons report on members for whom they have been concerned. Prayer is offered for God's special blessing.

At my church we see that the role of deacon is two-fold—vertical and horizontal. It is spiritual and social, relating to God and people.

We recently called a new staff member. The personnel committee recommended a candidate as a result of their interviews. The prospective staff member then met separately with the ministerial staff, support staff, educational staff, Church Council, and deacons. Each of these groups personally shared their observations and evaluations. However, only the church voted. This was done by secret ballot. Thus, we felt we could insist on the right of each member to be led by the Holy Spirit individually.

Partners in Ministry

Our church has a Deacon Family Ministry Plan. We have 60 active deacons and 1,200 resident families. Each deacon is assigned approximately 20 families.

We try to assign these geographically although it is simpler to assign them alphabetically. We feel it is more important for a deacon to be able to have easy access to his members. Otherwise, they may spend considerable amount of time crisscrossing the church field. At the beginning of each year we reassign all families. This means everyone starts off new.

We ask that each deacon make some contact with each family the first month. We suggest that he call or write each family and tell them who their new deacon is. We also ask each deacon to visit in each home of each family the first quarter. This will establish a personal identity. Names and faces can be put together and special needs can be noted. Then we encourage each deacon to follow up the rest of the year on an emergency basis. We feel special needs should dictate follow-up.

We encourage our deacons to give as much attention as they can to those they do not know. These are probably the inactive and incapacitated. These need the ministry of the church most. We try to put the most oil on the squeaking hinges.

When we learn of a special need, we do two things in the office. First, we call the deacon. Second, we send a card to the deacon. The call gives instant information to the deacon; the card we send assures accountability. We ask that the card be returned with the notation of results to be posted for follow-up. I have a whole desk drawer full of ministry cards that have been turned in. Scarcely does a service go by that at least one deacon does not give me a follow-up card.

Partners in Outreach

When someone first visits our church I make the first contact with them. I discover what their interests are and where they lived before they came to our area. I also seek to discover any needs that they may have or any previous experiences they have had in other churches.

This information I share with the staff, teachers, and deacons. Every week someone else is assigned to contact those whom I have contacted the previous week. Each week for the first month the ministerial staff follows up. Then I try to make a home visit. During the second month we ask the Sunday School classes and deacons to follow up.

The turn-around time for us is about two months. From the time of the initial visit until the person joins our church is about eight weeks. During these two months we can comprehensively communicate the ministry of the church to those who have visited us. Without overkill but with continuing contacts, we seek to get the church outside its four walls into the world where people are.

Dunwoody Baptist Church in Atlanta has a good program. Their deacons are divided into visitation teams. Each team is responsible for visiting on a certain Sunday afternoon each month those who have visited the church that morning. They plan short visits to answer any questions and invite the prospects to come back.

The no-show ratio is good. Most of those who have visited the church are at home. Few go out of town after attending church on a Sunday morning.

This visitation program powerfully communicates first and foremost the important role of the laity in the church. Deacons thus make the first contact, with the professional staff following up later.

The above suggestions are just a few of the ways that pastor and deacons can work together to help the church fulfill its mission. Deacons and pastor are called of God to be partners together in ministry. This exciting venture is worth our best efforts.

---

[1]From the Holy Bible, *New International Version,* copyright © 1973, 1978, 1984 by International Bible Society. Subsequent quotations are marked NIV.

Personal Learning Activities

Chapter 1

1. List and explain the three reasons that deacon leadership is essential.
2. Name the three ideals that best describe the biblical style of leadership for deacons.
3. What are some of the characteristics which the Bible expects of anyone desiring to lead?
4. Describe the eight biblical principles and models of leadership for deacons.
5. In what three ways do the deacons provide leadership?

Chapter 2

1. What are the four lessons to be learned from Acts 6?
2. How do we define ministry?
3. Through what ways may we do ministry?
4. Deacons should support the ministries of the church through what four ways?
5. Discuss the 10 deacon actions that can encourage a congregation to do ministry.

Chapter 3

1. The deacon minster must have two focuses. What are they?
2. What does it mean to be a leader in the community?
3. How are America's communities changing?
4. What are some of the deacon's roles in community leadership?

5. List and describe some community leadership-ministry projects in which you could be involved in your community?

Chapter 4

1. Changes stir up a diverse range of emotions in us. Congregations have to contend with many types of change. List some of these changes.
2. To manage change in a meaningful way, discuss how deacons can be a catalyst for change, how they can share information concerning change, and how they can be ready to accept change.
3. List and identify the four types of change and the three sources of change.
4. What are some reasons people are resistant to change and how do they respond to resistance? How does recognizing resistance help us deal with it?
5. Contrast right and wrong reasons for change.
6. Describe the eight keys to effective change.
7. What are the steps for planned change?
8. Deacons can serve as change agents, but they should have certain characteristics to help them in this role. What are they?

Chapter 5

1. What does *transition* mean?
2. One form of transition for a congregation is a change of pastors. What are some of the emotions felt by the congregation and by individuals when a pastor leaves?
3. What are the areas which deacons can help when the pastor leaves?
4. Another transition for a congregation is a changing community. What are the characteristics of a changing community?
5. Compare the stages in the life cycle of the community and the church.